# Sad Nun at Synanon

*barbara leslie austin*

# *Sad Nun at Synanon*

Holt, Rinehart and Winston, Inc.

New York Chicago San Francisco

Acknowledgment is made to the following for permission to reprint from their copyrighted works: Alfred A. Knopf, Inc., New York, N.Y. for excerpts from "Like Decorations in a Nigger Cemetery," copyright 1936 by Wallace Stevens; copyright renewed 1964 by Holly Stevens Stephenson. Reprint from BY THE NORTH GATE by Joyce Carol Oates by permission of the publisher, The Vanguard Press, Inc. Copyright © 1963, by Joyce Carol Oates.

Thank you to my editor, Joe Cunneen, for his unceasing help and encouragement; to Mary Callan Kiely for life and great joy; and to Sister Josephine and Sue Cota for all their help. And of course to the Synanon Foundation, Inc., for new eyes.


Published simultaneously in Canada by Holt, Rinehart and Winston of Canada, Limited.

Library of Congress Catalog Card Number 70–102150
First Edition

SBN: 03-084493-2
Designer: Marie Walborn
Printed in the United States of America

# Contents

*I dedicate this book*
*to my mom and dad,*
*and to the sisters (past and present)*
*in my religious community.*

*I only ask one question of them, "If everyone were a chalice—who would beg?"*

# 1.

# the shadow people

# Deep flutes in the Santa Monica sea

Nobody told me the fatigues. Nobody told me the temptations. When I took off my clogging black habit that day, there were no trumpets. All I possessed were my eagerness and my naiveté. The feeling of fear and pain hadn't yet washed to my bones. Now, thinking it over, it seems to me that the whole life of the Christian lies in sustaining this eagerness. The person who feels and has a keenness for life will know what I mean. But to the freezing and the frozen, my words will be a scandal.

Synanon has a phrase for people who see things only through their own prejudices: those who go through life listening to the sound of one hand clapping.

I ask Synanon to work upon them, as it did upon me: may it burn eyes in their hearts.

I came to Synanon a sad nun, stiff and embarrassed by my womanhood. My new clothes hung on me awkwardly, as if ashamed that they ended up there. And I left Synanon a sad nun, but clothed in a human grace.

I came to Synanon a young girl fed on silence, whose greatest joy was to dream and speak quietly of shining things. I came to Synanon believing I would become a most essential part of the Santa Monica sand; the sea would form my ears into shells so that wherever I went from then on, the sea could be heard—lapping, corroding, and balancing life on my middle ear.

I wonder, now, how a drug addict comes to Synanon. Surely not with dreams or inner stillness. With emptiness and yearning, yes—and I suppose, a certain anger. I came with none of these, but quickly found them there.

It is easier to live in a situation when you romanticize it. I romanticized Synanon because I was fearful of it. I knew nothing of sirens or knives, of small love-cries in the night; I had forgotten that I, too, am weak.

Did the sea of Synanon, its wave after wave of people, form my ears into gentle shells?

I began to listen to it the moment I sat with fourteen strangers in a circle. So this was the Synanon Game? Fourteen human beings with cigarettes poised and mouths ready to attack.

Someone asked me my name.

I answered, "Sister Barbara," although my name in religion was Sister Pierre. I lied because a few days previous when Sister Mary and I first arrived at Synanon, our apartment slip read: "to Kansas (Clumpette) apartments, #6—Sister Mary Marc and Sister Pierre (feminine) Austin." I didn't want them to have any illusions about my sex.

Someone huge asked me why I had come.

To serve, I told them.

They blew laughter out their noses and their mouths.

"What in the hell does a nun have to give us?"

"Yeah! Doesn't she live her name—none, nothing, *kaput*."

"Shit! We're goin' t'teach you baby, we're gonna socket t'ya." I smiled. They seemed inhibited. I had succeeded in spreading my stiffness.

"Goddamn—we're speaking softly to this asshole."

"Hey, nun! Have you been elated?"

This time I laughed, "Of course, I've been elated. Many times." Silence hardened around me. Their red eyes blinked me down.

Someone suddenly smiled and said, "You missed understood. I said laid."

"Yeah? Have you ever been laid?"

Somebody small and white added, "—You know, fucked." The stiffness crumpled. I laughed. Here I was only twenty-two-years-old and acting like my habit had smothered me! Hadn't I gone to public school for nine years? Hadn't I dated right up until I was nineteen? All the books that I had read, the movies I'd seen—

"No," I said quietly. "I'm a virgin."

This threw them off their chairs. Laughter coughed and blurted out every hole in their bodies.

"Whatsa virgin?"

"I thought that went out with Mary!"

"Hey! What's the worse thing y've ever done?"

I gulped. "Well." I looked around the small, bare room. "Are you ready for it?" I said.

They moved forward in their chairs.

"Well—" I gulped again, and covered my face with my hands. "I—I—I stole a mantilla once!"

They stayed off their chairs this time. They were mine now. At least for a little while, we were one in laughter. And I began to glean a little of their hostility toward the Church, their stereotyped boredom at the thought of a nun, and perhaps, a glint of the guilt.

Of course, I could not see my guilt then. At that time, I was too interested in things: persons, shells, silence. They hadn't opened me yet. I couldn't see, couldn't hear the deep flutes in the Santa Monica sea.

# The first hoopla

April, 1968. I called her up. "Sister Mary," I began. "My civics teacher's manual says we should be more involved in urban problems. I've already taken my students to the newspaper and police station."

"So?" she answered.

"Well, let's go down to Synanon. We could bring back a lot of information for our students."

So we got into a community car and drove up to Santa Monica; we were going to a Synanon Saturday Night Open House, long black habits and all.

An ex-addict named John Nicholas greeted us at the door and gave us a grand tour of the Club: we took in the large ballroom and dining room, the renovated bar called "The Data Lounge," and the hundreds of people milling about.

A man spoke into a microphone on the stage, "Now, the Sounds of Synanon Band will do—the Hoopla." Everyone cheered.

John explained that the Hoopla was like a tribal dance, where everyone got into long lines and danced in the same direction, "while doing their own thing. It's Synanon's whole life-style, Sisters, only danced out."

I understand. Kazantzakis' *Zorba the Greek* was one of my favorite books. I understood about dancing, even if I didn't dance.

I smiled at John while quietly stilling my own feet, and felt my tongue salivate as he lit another cigarette. "I teach eighth-grade civics," I began, "and need to meet people who are involved in urban problems."

John stared at me, his face twitching nervously. "I can't talk about 'urban problems,' Sister—but I can run you my own story. It was one I used to be ashamed of. Now I'm hopeful."

So he ran his story, and there was great fascination and wonder as we heard how Synanon took John's dying life and made it passionate again.

"Sure—I was dying. I had been in the thirty-day cure-all

drug hospitals so many times, and fifteen minutes after I was out, I would meet a connection and have the good needle in me.

But I was getting old. I had so many felony convictions that the judge wrote me down on the books as a hopeless addict. Bullshit. They pretend drug addiction's a disease, treating it with white hospitals, nurses, and pills. They pull you off one trip to put you on another. They never realize (because they've never been one of us) that it's not a disease, but a person. A disordered person, that's what I am. I need order."

Listening to John, I watched the hundreds of people laughing and talking in the Data Lounge. It was amazing to see so many adults enjoying themselves without liquor.

"So I go to my twenty-five-an-hour (paid by the taxpayers, of course) psychiatrist and he tells me, 'John, look, I can't help you. You've got what they call an addictive personality.' The psychiatrist pats his heavy belly. 'I'm fifty pounds overweight,' he says, 'I can't get rid of my addiction to food, I don't know how to help you get rid of your addiction to drugs.' So what am I to do now? I'm a disordered person with an addictive personality." He smiles.

The Hoopla is playing again. Old thoughts run back to me. Dancing. Men. Haven't been in an atmosphere like this since entering the convent. I can feel that Sister Mary is watching me. She wants to dance. No, I shake my head.

John is saying, "So I decide to go to England where addiction is pretty well accepted. I mean, I know I'm going to die. There's no such thing as an old addict."

"Really?" I mutter.

"Yeah. You know, you'll die by violence, one way or another."

"Overdose?" Mary suggests.

"Shit no, Sister. Excuse me—" His craggy face blushes. "Hepatitis, maybe, gunned down when the heat's on—that kind of stuff. But not overdose. A hard dope fiend knows how to take his stuff. That's what so fine about heroin—once you're on it, you never have a bad trip—except when you run out."

"You mean, you don't shake and have a violent reaction when you're kicking it?" I ask.

"Hell no. It's like, well, a light flu. When I take you out of the Club to your car, you'll see some people that are kicking.

We put them right on sofas in the sitting room of the Club."

"Isn't that cruel?" Mary wonders, "to have everyone watch them?"

"That's the point. The social workers, parole officers, doctors, psychiatrists, do a great job of babying the addict. That's where I was at when I decided to go to England. Then I heard of Synanon, so I visited it. After five minutes of talking, I knew this was the place. For the first time I was with people who knew me. We spoke the same lingo. When I said 'snow' they knew it, baby."

"Snow?"

"Dope. So I stayed. Been here two and a half years. Work as a driver for the Medical section of Synanon (taking people to and from doctors and hospitals); I'm trusted but not babied."

Back at the convent after our visit to Synanon, I sat quietly for a long time. Ambivalent feelings. First of all, I felt that what Synanon and I believed were very close indeed. Wasn't Synanon trying to awaken human beings to a deeper sense of life?

It seemed to me, at that time, that a child comes into life with his feet caked with dreams. Reality helps clean his feet a little but nothing can rid him of his need to be in touch with all parts of life, the things that are and the things to come. Today's alienation, whether expressed individually in drug addiction, promiscuity, and violence, or corporately, in riots and wars, are all ways of dancing out our anguish. Synanon offered a way of spewing out this anguish in the torn shreds of words so that we could be free to dream again, together.

Secondly, Synanon seemed to be on the right track for salvation. To me this meant becoming more completely conscious and sensitive to one's fellowman. It meant to have people in this world who are unafraid, full of hope, willing to reveal their weakness and their strength, and willing, ultimately, to serve.

But, somehow, I felt an aura of fear surrounding Synanon. And when Sister Mary wanted to go back to the next Saturday Night Open House, I tried to conjure up excuses, but none came. So I went with her and met Jack Hurst, Executive President of the Synanon Foundation, and Dr. Disselor, director of Medical Operations.

Jack took our hands warmly. "We need you. Would you like to teach at our School?"

I almost passed out. "School?"

"Yes, for the children of our residents. We need professional teachers. Would you be interested?"

Sister Mary grabbed my arm. "When?"

Jack smiled. "This summer. Only two things that we ask—one, that you live as residents; and two, that you don't wear your habits."

Dr. Disselor laughed. "After all, we don't allow the Black Muslims theirs!" He looked at me a moment. "You will have nothing to lose, you know, Sister—you might gain something if the Pope will let you come."

I laughed. "Pope? Well, we'll ask our Superior, Doctor. You might be right. We just might gain something."

The band began to play. Sister Mary and I looked at each other. Yes. We went out on the floor to dance the Hoopla.

# Keep those damn nuns away from our kids

Sister Mary and I shivered on our dead seats in front of Al Bauman, director of the Synanon School. He had once been a concert pianist and was always involved in education. He and his wife had been in Synanon for two years. He was a "square" (not an addict) and had come to be a resident for the social movement, not for rehabilitation.

His blue eyes unclogged us both. His first words, like our discarded habits, hung in the air—

"Do you know what the old man said when he heard two nuns were coming to teach at Synanon?"

"First, tell us who's the 'old man,' " I said softly, fearful that his words might fall.

"Charles E. Diedrich (Chuck), the founder of Synanon. In '58 he was a hopeless drunk wallowing in the Santa Monica sand. He had wrecked his college career and a couple of marriages. Had tried A.A. but it wasn't strong enough for him. He needed total-environmental help, not just a chance to get a little peer backup once a week or on the telephone. So he did two things—he went on a controlled L.S.D. experience at U.C.L.A. and got a little inner illumination; and he began to read Emerson."

"Emerson?" I asked. It surprised me more than the L.S.D. Didn't he know that Emerson was passé? Utopian?

"Yes, he began to believe in self-reliance. So he got some money together and found a small place to begin. He got a few other alcoholics to join him and they began to work on each other."

"That's how the Games started?" Mary asked.

"Yes. They began as gripe sessions and gradually became the gut level situations they are today. They let people act out their feelings in a verbal way instead of in hostile, anti-social acts. Anyway, Chuck soon found that his idea worked as well for drug addicts as alcoholics. So Synanon grew. They moved to the Old Armory on Pacific Coast Highway soon after, and lived there until just a few months ago, when we got the old Del Mar Beach Club. We've been enlarging by leaps. The School's an example."

"The name—Synanon?"

"Some dingbat couldn't say seminar, the name we give for a lecture-discussion by one of our older residents, and said 'Synanon' instead."

Oh felix malaprop! "Well, what did Chuck say about us?" I asked.

"When he heard you two were coming to teach, all he said was: *Keep those damn nuns away from our kids.*"

I looked at Mary—why? Did we come to be insulted? Al continued quietly, "Unlike myself, a Jew, Chuck was once a Catholic."

Damn, I thought to myself, why can't we go anywhere without being branded "The Church" in neon letters? What's the point of representing the Church when it aches like this?

"So you two summer escapees from the nunnery—"

"It's *not* a nunnery," Mary said emphatically. "A nunnery sounds like some cannery. And you'll see, Al—the products aren't the same, maybe the labels are, but—"

"Well, *Sisters,* just remember you're not at Synanon to be our savior-teachers," Al interrupted. "You're coming into a school where we are more interested in the style of relating, the process, than the facts. A school in which *you* must establish the environment for learning. The thrust is sharing: we, the learners, must question ourselves much more in every area, not simply question the children. It has to do with establishing a quality of taste."

"What do you mean?" I asked.

"Let's assume that the child is born perfect, ready to cope with himself and his world. But as he travels through his environment, he often becomes sick, disoriented. What we hope to do is establish an environment where the child can grow into a conscious totality. And the quality that you, a demonstrator of learning, can give is one of taste: to show how a functioning mind creates alternatives."

Mary nods. "Yes, I like that."

"What's the environment you set up, Al?" I asked.

"We are on a Perpetual Stew at the School, which means an extended Game. After the child has gotten out all the shit that has been building up in him, after he breaks down some of that hostility, we send him up to a workroom to share the learning process with a demonstrator." He smiled at us. "Like Synanon, our subject matter at the School is human existence. Above everything else, we ourselves are the subject we teach." He waited a moment. Lit another cigarette slowly. "You must learn to use your subject matter."

So I said to him, "What will you have us do?"

"Your job, Mary and Barbara, is to be demonstrators. You're going to show the kids how to learn. I'm the schoolmaster here, but I don't pretend to be the giant administrative mind. All I do (and it's damn hard) is show others that I'm *learning* how to be a schoolmaster. I know how to ask questions and approximately where to find answers. But most of all, I've learned how to use those answers once I've found them. That's all a human being needs to grow and become full and give. Your Church has no prerogative on giving."

"We never said it did, Al. No such claim was ever written down in our lesson plan," I answered.

"There are no lesson plans at this school, Barbara. Out of your fullness you'll give, not out of the plentitude of your preparations. Now—what are you interested in learning about? What gives you joy in studying, Mary?"

She clears her throat. "Well, I love correlating theology and modern literature; also, writing."

"Sounds interesting but we don't need it this summer. How about demonstrating how to study comparative religions and sharing it with our seven-to-fourteen-year-old group?"

"Okay, I guess," she gulped, and smiled at me.

"And you, Barbara?"

(*And you, Andrew Marvell?* I thought), "Many things. Learning to be a poet; I'd like to know the names of birds, butterflies—bats. To look for shells: to use the ocean. And myths. For me, seeing life is a mythology. And stars. I've never seen the Big Dipper before, although I've strained my eyes looking."

"Why didn't you see it?" he asked.

"People have tried to point it out. But I've got to find it myself."

"Fine. Let's see you spend your time in your workshops (*not* classroom) learning how to be a naturalist-mythologist. There's an interesting polarity between those two disciplines. Perhaps later, you'll scrape your head against a star."

# Old holy cards and new stars

It all started when they changed the holy cards. Once they had been delicately pink and ornate with an abundance of gold angels, haloed saints, and Holy Marys everywhere. Then they suddenly became more American and less gold-lined. Instead of vellum paper, they were printed on plastic, with bright colors in geometric shapes; instead of a bearded Father-figure, God became a triangle. There were less quotes from the saints, less indulgences, and more pericopes from the Bible.

At first, not understanding the change, I was uneasy. I had a sneaking suspicion that the God of the Green Triangle belonged on a dollar bill, not a holy card. After all, hadn't I become a Catholic to find peace? I loved the Latin Masses and my huge brown leather missal. I loved the votive lights twitching by the altar of God, each one symbolizing someone who needed assistance. That is why I became a Sister—for all those who lit ten-cent votive candles and waited on bended knee for an answer. But then the sun became for me a more priceless votive light: the world needs help, the world needs an answer, it blinked to the bland sky.

So I entered the convent at nineteen. I met Mary Marc there, and together we spent three years growing up nun. After our first six months, we were received as novices and began our canonical year. Of all the good years in my life, the one during which I wore the white novice veil is the most precious memory. I sat on the rim of myself the whole time; my head was shaved and the fat all worked off me. I prayed so many hours that my knees and my soul were getting love-calluses. We were very poor in that Novitiate in Santa Barbara, but rich in laughter and time to find each other and God. I made my deepest friendships that year. And God was in my eyes; he was part of my walk; when I bent down to pick up dust or pull rose garden weeds, he rode my back, not a cross but a joy. Then the holy cards changed, and with them the whole Church.

After that, it was goodbye to a nice, safe convent life, and hello, world. But that novice year, that innocent white-veiled year, gave me a residue of peace as a preparation for reality. Just prior to our coming to Synanon, I wrote this poem for Mary. Little did I realize how accurate it would stand as prophecy.

How we relished it, you and I! How weary,
Worry, tiresome days sagged from us—
Naked white veils, we anticked in blameless
Ways the guideless wind! Had we known
Of serpents and visions to come: had we known
Of Godravishments, the inrush of joy?

Naked and bright we could not grasp—
The black sigh of night.

Some giant votive candle in the sky must have enflamed Pope John XXIII to call his Ecumenical Council. Whatever it was that prodded him, by the time Sister Mary and I were finally stamped by the giant communal hand as "ready for service," we were sent out to a new religious life working in a more realistic Church.

In my holy card stage, life had seemed a very sweet, Jesus-and-the-stable place. As I progressively tossed my holy cards and my brown leather missal away, and took up the Bible and the business of being more human, it became increasingly clear that all of life is a process of death and resurrection. The more I stuck my black nun-shoe-being into things, the more I died, and consequently, the more I came alive.

Witness our permission to come to Synanon. It was an extraordinary sign of trust because Sister Mary and I had only been teaching for one year. I made up my mind to accept that trust, to return to my convent no matter what, so that my experiences would not be wasted, but rather could be used to enrich us all. It was an opportunity for resurrection, and consequently, one of death—I found out that Sister Mary was planning to leave our Order as soon as our Synanon summer was over.

It is painful to scrape your head against a star. Let me use an outrageous metaphor to describe Synanon: A star has a very wide center with five points enamating from it. The center of Synanon is the Club (1900 Ocean Front Avenue in Santa Monica), and issuing from its center are five extensions: the Clump (a street of apartments on Cloverfield Boulevard), the Clumpette (a street of apartments on Pico Boulevard), Synanon Industries (producing Synanon pencils and pens, notebooks, etc.) and Gas Station on Pico Boulevard, Synanon Market and Supply Center (which are only for resident use) in Venice, and the Synanon School one block from the Club, directly in back of Muscle Beach.

The School consisted of two decaying beach houses. The bottom of one was used for the children's Stew room, where the forty or so in the seven-to-thirteen-year-old group met at nine each morning and spent a while releasing their hostilities, or more colloquially, *getting the shit out.* Along one side of this large room was a "grazing table," fixed with punch, fruit, sandwiches, and soup the children could eat at any time. A kitchen and Al's office were also on this floor; upstairs was the library and various workshops for the demonstrators.

The bottom floor of the other house was for the five-to-six-year-old group. It had an old wood floor and wide windows, so that you were consistently aware of the bathing beauties outside. My workshop was upstairs, directly above the five-to-six-year-olds' Stew and play room. How I loved to begin each morning with the euphonious sound of contented children screaming, "You did! Goddamn it, you stole my green socks!"

"Bullshit, he's got my pants on!"

Then the demonstrators and Game leaders, Terry and Louanne, would interject, "Did you steal it, Joannie?"

"Yes, she stole it, I was with her."

"You liar, you fuckhead, you assbowl," etc.

How I liked my workshop in that old house. It had one tall window that could be kept open with one well-placed brick. When studying, there was the sea wind on my neck, and I could hear the swallows. No wonder there was only one window, the house was full of holes; for the first time in my life, I could hear the ancient cooing of the seabirds. Somehow their cooing made me incomprehensibly sad. But after all, life itself is full of holes: the nearest image to being is a butterfly net.

I laid my newly acquired book, *The Amateur Naturalist,* on the table. The first chapter was "Observing Animals," so I decided to observe the nearest animal, the swallow. I got some paper, sharpened a pencil, and strolled through my workshop into the nearby weaving room. I, too, had something to weave . . .

> why's the swallow's toes raspberry?
> what does he do with that turned-down beak?

Aphrodite lives by the ocean. She lives on the second floor of a geranium-laden, windburnt house. She reads the newspaper near her man each day at 9 A.M. She is an aurora-child. Clean-Thoreau-living, with each day a perpetual morning. She spends her love discovering. And when her eyelids become heavy with newspaper grime and book dirt, she pulls on her bodyshades and goes out to build sandcastles. The sand wears away the rough edges of her sadness—for even Aphrodite gets sad—and very gradually, she becomes as smooth and warm as old colored glass or pebbles at the edge of the sea. When she tires of walking, she—

"Hi, Sister Barbara! Watcha doin'?" Two ten-year-olds. They must have been sent up to me from the Stew.

"Oh, Oh, hi!" My eyes smile. "Watching the swallows." I pull out my notebook. "See?" I point to my illustrations. "I've drawn their bills and feet and now—"

They're both laughing. Bermudas, tennis shoes, and tanned faces, all laughing on top of me. One of them puts his hand easily on my shoulder.

"*Those* aren't swallows!" He howls and points outside. "Pigeons! They're pigeons!"

What could I do? What could I say? There were no holy cards left for me to grab onto; I joined in their laughter.

# Sand in the crevasse of the celebration

I came to Synanon armed with quite a few misapprehensions. One of them was that the children at the School would be slow.

My students at the convent school in Palos Verdes came to my fifth-grade class with a rich verbal and cultural background. Their median I.Q. was 115; three children were over 130. To my surprise, the sons and daughters of drug addicts proved just as curious and alert. Frankly, the class was more exciting, because I never had to waste time disciplining them.

Imagine a teaching situation in which children freely listened without pinching, talking, or passing notes. The children's Game (the Stew) really enabled them to get rid of their hostilities and frustrations before they came to learn. It also gave them a unique opportunity to confront an inadequate teacher for being boring, unprepared, or unfair.

Synanon doesn't teach in the usual methods. When a drug addict or a square enters the Club they don't waste time telling them, "Our impetus is very Emersonian and based on the belief that there comes a time in everyone's life when a man arrives at the conviction that once a man accepts himself, he will continue to grow and develop his potentialities. As long as he does not accept himself, much of his energies will be used to defend rather than to explore and actualize himself" (from *The Synanon Philosophy*); rather, they invite the newcomers to experience that process of learning which is the Game. There a person sees how he defends rather than explores; he receives a graphic demonstration that "a man is relieved and gay when he has put his heart into his work and done his best; but what he has said or done otherwise shall give him no peace [ibid.]." Synanon doesn't tell a new resident or member to read this book, or catch this movie, or hear this record and *then* you'll understand. All they say is live here awhile, take the wax out of your life, and become a full man or woman by listening or participating in another's growth (the Game).

McLuhan go mad: Synanon is the message.

All of Synanon exemplifies what Al Bauman told Mary and me about education. It is the environment, the life-style of learning, that changes people. And Synanon has the possibilities to make learning come about—

> No one can force a person towards permanent or creative learning. He will learn only if he wills to. Any other type of learning is temporary and inconsistent with the self and will disappear as soon as the threat is removed. Learning is possible in an environment that provides information, the setting, materials, resources, and by his being there [*ibid.*].

Actually, I had two lives at Synanon—my life at the School and my life at the Club.

I'd get up in time to walk to St. Anne's Church six blocks away; after Mass, I'd run back to the Clump to catch the jitney and get to school in time to hear the little kids yell *assbowl* in their Game below. Then an hour or two studying mythology or natural science, still without breakfast, since I never got up in time for the 6:30 A.M. shift at the Club. After that, four or five children would be sent out of the Stew to me. It was up to them whether they would stay an hour or all day. I'd try a little of everything with them. If it was mythology we were doing, first, I would tell them the story. They seemed to like the myths of Hermes, Hercules, and Apollo the best. Then we'd act it out in a play, or write a poem about the myth, or if I had some seven- or eight-year-olds, we'd draw pictures. For the first time, I saw it was possible to teach an eight-year-old with a twelve-year-old. One day, after we had learned about Hermes, we even invited Nicky Salant, a five-year-old from Terry's group, to play Hermes as we acted out his famous argument with his brother, Apollo.

In teaching natural science, I used the beach as my main place of activity. Unhappily, there wasn't much sea life left at Santa Monica, so we took field trips. I took Charlene, Susan, Kenny, and Alex up to Will Rogers Park, where we spent the day joyfully searching for lizards. Another time, I took Nora, Peter, and Kenny Hurst down to the Tide Pools in Palos Verdes.

My school day began at 9 A.M. and ended about 5 P.M. The worst times were when I had three or four of the same children all day in my small workshop. After five, Mary and I would try to get in a few moments of prayer, quiet conversation, or reading. Then came dinner, and our second life at Synanon would begin. Until the Games began at 8 P.M., most residents sat in the Data Lounge and talked to each other, the square Game members, and visitors.

I played the Game three times a week. Monday nights, I played with the directors of Synanon and their wives, P.R. people, important square Game players, and various visitors.

Thursday afternoons, I played as the only square, except Sister Mary, with a regular resident tribe, the Titans, all of whom were in Synanon for help. And Wednesday nights, I played with the Mamas and Papas, one of the most active tribes in the Club. They were predominantly square, non-resident Club members, but a few residents also (Al and Nina Bauman and Nancy Clark) played the Games. What most had in common was that they were the mothers and fathers of children who had been on dope, pills, or pot before coming to Synanon. To give these children growth and time to get used to the environment, the parents were not allowed to speak to them for three months. The rule was strictly observed. Many of the parents joined the tribe simply because they wanted to be able to see their child. But one Santa Barbara man, whose son was at Synanon in San Diego, drove all the way to Santa Monica every Wednesday night just to play the Game.

The Mamas' and Papas' tribe was a perceptive idea. Many of those kids (teenagers and olders) would eventually return to their home environment and it would be a lot easier to have a mother and father who had grown up when they got there.

So Synanon was feeding me too much stimuli. I felt slightly devoured; those first interminable weeks were horrible. Here, there was no time and no solitude. Mary and I had barely unraveled our crumpled sleep sheets when the work began. Even when I was awake for them, Mass and meditation were mostly one anguished psalm,

> is not all talk where anguish is?
> is not life all verbal honks and spugs?
> is not death all asphalt and work?

The poet is a microscope. A lens so delicate that coupled with another lens, one sees way below matter to life. And life is a lonely thing, of many movements: a flagella, an amoeba, and plankton. There are those who feed and are fed. And there are those who are devoured.

It was unfortunate that I chose the microscopes to begin with—the children loved them. And since there were no bells, no joyous free periods for Spanish and coffee breaks, gym and recess, I'd have those kids with me four hours running. I felt like a question box; they were so eager.

Sister Mary was moved to the Nursery. It was almost impossible to teach comparative religions to seven-to-fourteen-year-olds with no text, visual aids, or lesson plan.

Finally, I complained. I strutted into Al's office, forgetting I was no longer a penguin, and planted myself on the hot seat.

"Ah—'Tis our Synanun." He laughed. "Did you get the third microscope?"

"How should I know?" I growled. "Unless some kid has it stuck to his eyeball!"

"Tut. Learning getting you down, Sister?"

"Yes, I miss my routine," I answered.

He looked out the window to the people walking by on the beach promenade. "You'll get used to it."

I slammed my hand down on the arm of my chair. "But the hours? By three o'clock my mouth is full of cotton, my eyes are myopic, my back is a screw."

He smiled carefully. "I see you're picking up our language."

"Very funny," I answered slowly, "but don't you think it's too much for the kids? How can they assimiliate after four hours straight? It's been proven that a person's attention span—"

"Nice cop-out, Barbara. Don't blame your inadequacies on the children's, quote, 'inabilities.' I will tell you two things. First, here at Synanon, we don't go by the so-called 'experts.' The experts say drug addiction is incurable. So the drug addicts talk themselves into the belief that they've got an incurable disease, and they die. Until Synanon, that is. The experts say a four-year-old child has an attention span of about four and a half minutes. But here at our Nursery, Thad has held discussions with those children about Vietnam for over an hour."

"But—"

He lit another cigarette and ran the palm of his hand up his forehead and over his bushy, gray hair. "Here at Synanon, we believe in infinite possibilities. And we have the enclosed environment to experiment with our existence. Time, for instance. Why does man use only the day for his work? Once it was a physical necessity; now that idea's absurd. Why does man think he can only work eight hours a day? Why not try ten or twelve? Why not expand one of our two-hour Games to five, six, twenty-four hours? Or why not have it for seventy-two? That's what our cubic day idea is all about!"

"Cubic day?" I said weakly, wishing I had a cigarette.

"Instead of a twenty-four-hour day, we have a twenty-four-day cycle. For fourteen days a person is put on *motion,* which means he works at least ten to fourteen hours a day."

I made a face.

"It's possible, Barbara," he went on. "Then he goes into *pressure,* or a seventy-two-hour Stew. After that, he goes into an eight-day *vacuum,* which is re-creation."

"Re-creation? Sounds biblical."

"Sorry." His eyes crinkled when he laughed. "It's eight days when a person has time to read or go to the beach or try art. And interestingly enough, it's not the *motion* or the *pressure* that gets people down, but the *vacuum.* After the first few days, boredom sets in. What to do with yourself without sex, liquor, drugs? We want to use all twenty-four hours. We have Dennis Resino working on Tesserect, that is, putting all our 800 people on a twenty-four-hour timetable, so that our plant is continually active."

"It sounds tremendous, Al. But I know what to with my time. Why don't you give me a little *vacuum?*" I asked.

"We'd like to expand your possibilities a little, too. I thought we were getting a nun—I thought nuns worked a twenty-four-hour day."

"Sorry. Not this nun, Al. A person needs time to breathe. I'm so tired when I get home, I can't even pray or watch the news."

"Tut—tut. Can't even pray?" He smiles. "You'll toughen."

I got up to leave, thinking that there are two types of whys—one is the why of the wave, the other is the why that is sand.

That day, there was sand in the crevasse of the celebration. I huffed outside. Two of the five-and-six-year-old group were playing quietly by the old, empty swimming pool. Randy, a little guy with scarecrow hair, smiled up at me. He was writing his name on a clean sheet of paper. I sat down beside him.

It calmed me to see him struggle with the difficult N. Yet I felt like pigeons were inside, crudding my peace. Michelle, a very petite, dark-haired five-year-old finally noticed me.

"Whatsa nun?" she said as she stood up.

I gulped. Oddly, embarrassed, I tried a definition: "A nun is someone who works for God."

She jabs me, "*God is dead, baby!*"

What do you do when life hits you between the eyes? All I could do was laugh. I almost rolled into the pool, I was laughing so hard. I unraveled myself from the clump of Randy and Michelle. Hugging the latter, I took the flight of stairs in about three leaps, got my gear, hopped onto a jitney, and rushed back to the Nursery in the Kansas Clump. Mary was changing diapers; when I told her about Al, she seconded my anguish. Then with tears of laughter running down my face, I told her about Michelle.

"But Barb," Mary asked soberly, "does Michelle *believe* it?"

O Mary, my sister, my friend! God sends his messengers and we are Job. The second lens of the poet is people. People and the poet's sense make joy. No time to write life as we'd like it. So much of Synanon, of life as people live it, is interminable absorption.

# The black sigh of night

In L.A., Persephone decided to change her covenant. She told her mother, Demeter, that she'd prefer to stay in Hell two-thirds of the time with Pluto, rather than live in L.A.

So we get Demeter's freeway anger most of the year. She spews out smog, while the dark couple laugh. Surely, the anger was real as I rode with Vicki by the Kansas Clump. Vicki is a square who teaches art at the School; she was explaining what she was doing in her class when I noticed a cohort of blacks thudding down the sidewalk, their young faces simmering with ancient resentment. Suddenly, one of them began to hit a small, newly planted tree outside an apartment. Our car passed him, and he looked up and caught my eye. Then he deliberately took the tree in his hands and ripped it in two.

"Look at that guy," I yelled.

Vicki slammed on the brakes. "What?"

"Why, he's tearing that tree in two!" I answered, starting to open the door, but Vicki grabbed my arm.

"Don't do it," she said quietly, and started the car.

I looked at her in disbelief.

"Just think how'd you feel," she explained.

"Good God," I said righteously, "even if I were angry, I wouldn't abuse someone else's property."

Vicki smiled. "Have you ever experienced poverty, Barbara?"

"If you mean poverty as environment, no, but I've known other sorts of poverty."

We waited at a stop light. Her glance was a question.

"The poverty of my abilities, for instance. One poverty I feel bad about is my mom."

"What do you mean by that?"

"Well, Vicki, once I saw an old picture album of hers. There was one picture I especially liked; she was standing outdoors with the wind brushing her hair across her face."

"What has that got to do with the price of beans?" she laughed.

I looked at her a moment. "Well, I would have liked to be a part of her life when she was young and the hair brushed against her face like that—before I came along, dragging her down."

"All right, Barb," she smiled again, "so you have your own small sadness. Everybody does. So?"

"Yes," I said quietly, "you're right. There's a greater sadness."

"Yes?"

"Well, it's what you reminded me a while ago—'Think how they feel'—Well, if I can't even see into my own mother, how can I see into anyone else?"

"That's the point. Can you imagine how it is for a black on Pico Boulevard? Do you have any perception into it now?

I looked straight ahead. "One small door in my mind wants to open. That's all."

The same smog and anger were all about us as John Nicholas and I stepped out of the Synanon car in the center of L.A. We were going to visit Doug at the L.A. County Hospital. He was in the old wing, set aside for the old, the poor, and the wicked, brought together by their lack of dollars.

The ward was hot, green, and dirty. Doug looked tired and there was a small hole in his top sheet. He was only nineteen but had to have a hernia operation; he'd been working in the Synanon Gas Station and breaking his insides. Conversation was awkward; Doug told us that two of the guys in his ward had been shot. I looked over at one. He was much bigger than Doug, and surrounded by three young men, two of them wearing faded leather jackets with *The Vultures* stitched on the back. Two girls were there, too, but it was obvious that he really wanted to be left alone.

Suddenly, I became aware of soft groans, just across from me. It was an old twig of a man, strapped to a low bed whose face was a spider's web caught on the twig. His mouth rolled convulsively, "I'm sorry, I'm sorry, I'm sorry."

I held a corner of Doug's sheet in my hands. Slowly, as if keeping time with the old man, I rolled it back and forth.

"Sir?" I said. I wondered if it would have been easier if I

were wearing my habit, if seeing a nun might have been reassuring to him.

"I'm sorry, I'm sorry." He tried to sit up in bed.

"Is there anything I can do?" I whispered.

"Waiting, waiting, waiting."

The nurse came in, and gruffly motioned for me to move. I went back to Doug's bed and held onto the sheet again. Back and forth, it rolled in my hands. I no longer watched the old man, and was relieved when John announced it was time to go.

As we walked slowly out of the ward, I thought of the Santa Monica Hospital where I had worked for two summers—antiseptic, flowers everywhere. And didn't these people need flowers? There are so many places to breathe life. But how?

How? I whispered to myself as we rode back on the low freeway. I began to play my usual game—counting the car-pains of others, thinking about life to do, people to build, hopes to hoopla, dreaming in the hot smell and smog of the city.

John asked me if I had any questions about Synanon, but I hadn't formed my questions yet. I was only waiting, strapped up like the old twig-man, trying to get the feel of the people and the place.

"You're quiet, aren't you?" John broke in on my thoughts.

No one had ever said that to me before. He told me he thought Mary talked a lot.

I smiled. "But she's really the quieter one."

"She makes me talk like I've never talked," John said. "I've never felt the same way after speaking with a person. Good. I feel clean."

I was grateful for what John said about Sister Mary, grateful yet embarrassed. Why had I not learned the human way of talking and of fumbling, the healing way? When a voice moans in the city, and others, slowly, painfully, respond to that need, a psalm begins.

Demeter's smog and anger were still with me as I got back to the Club; there in the main dining room was a very thin, lonely boy. His hair was so neatly done, I almost thought he was a girl. I brought my food over and sat beside him. He had such long lashes, I could see dust on their ends, and his teeth came together delicately. I thought of him suddenly on a precipice, not knowing which way to turn.

I introduced myself. He saw that I was reading Kazantzakis' *Report to Greco*. He seemed interested so I read him a passage which I had savored, and had made my own secret. After it was over, he looked at me softly and began running his story. It was all L.A. and loneliness. How he had shot speed since he was seventeen and was completely dependent on it. He would get up at six for his job as an orderly at a hospital in Hollywood, shoot his speed, work until about three, and shoot some more in the antiseptic hospital bathroom—this would keep him going until eleven or twelve at night. The only time he would remember to eat was when he smoked grass. Then he would get hungry, and could sleep. On the average, he got three hours of sleep a night until Synanon.

I didn't know what to say. "How old?"

"I'm twenty, Sister."

"Would you like *Report to Greco*?" I asked, wondering why I was so tense and foreign.

He took the book and left me with a dull emptiness. Helpless, I wondered what would happen to him. Suddenly, it seemed that if I got deeply into Synanon, I might give up searching the stars, reading myths, and perhaps, even my need to pray so much.

Maybe Synanon was Demeter's freeway. What was sure was my fears and my inadequacies. I couldn't understand those blacks, or help the old twig-man, or reach this speed-fiend, or even speak to John. All I had was one small door in my mind, creaking.

# A miracle, please

I'm the sort of person who keeps eating until the table's pulled away from me. Jelly doughnuts, cokes and chocolate, preferably, but if pressed, I'll settle for coffee ice cream cones, french fries, and hamburgers. This was my menu at Synanon. Unaccustomed to our new freedom, Mary and I were continually missing dinners. Fortunately, we received two dollars WAM (walk-around-money) a week. Before coming to Synanon, we had discussed how we'd give the money to the poor; now we were the poor. Or so I believed. Once, I saw Mary give her money to the collection plate on Sunday; I read my missal and let the plate pass.

I'm also the sort of person who can let my body fall from me. Playing the part of the nun was rather enjoyable—being the fourth person who doesn't fit into the Mr./Mrs./Miss pattern. Synanon says it better: "You know, man, woman, and nun." I rather liked my neutership. After the tree-tearing incident with Vicki, I could walk down Pico Boulevard and be only eyes and ears and, perhaps, hands. I could be the Mexican or the Negro if I wanted—anything, so long as I could eat and talk, and forget the pain for a while.

I suppose it's the sense of being on the edge of things. Of owning everything because you have nothing—not even the sense of yourself, which is the greatest property. I read Thoreau diligently those first lonely weeks; even told Dan Marsh of the Oversoul tribe I'd do a cerebration with his people on Thoreau. That was all to change, but at that time I carried Thoreau's phrase, "A man is rich in proportion to the number of things which he can afford to let alone," as if it were a cross.

For there was pain. I had not expected Synanon to be a subculture, complete with its own language—

indictments (accusations in a Game)

dropping a lug (a very heavy criticism given in a Game)

acting out (to act out feelings in an anti-social manner, e.g. drinking, shooting dope, etc.)

making a contract (to make a pact with someone prior to a Game in which you both decide to protect one another)

splitting (to break off all contact with Synanon), etc.

My head tingled with its words.

Nor was I prepared for the constant changes. For instance, at Synanon a bald head indicated a public act of penance, imposed on an addict who had tried to split, or taken a woman, or used drugs again. But the idea got reversed while I was there, after two ex-addicts named Portie and Richie were forceably removed from Synanon because they refused to take the Naline Test (medical examination by authorities from Corona State Hospital to see if they were still on drugs). Since they had been paroled by the court from Corona to Synanon, the authorities had this prerogative, but Synanon felt that such a test, given to two persons who were clean, was an affront to their human dignity.

Chuck Diedrich sent word from his brain trust in Tomales Bay that a bald head would no longer be a punishment but a demonstration of the Synanon life-style, and of sympathy for the plight of Portie and Richie. He also said he wanted to see three thousand bald heads in California, resident and square. Along with the men, all the resident women got their hair cut very short. I refused: only once had I done such a thing, and it was for God.

The ferment of improvisation and fluidity bothered me: they'd change whole areas of the Club (knock out walls, redo floors) in two days, remove all the chairs in a tribe room and replace them with new ones, reshuffle workrooms, or change the head of the School and most of its staff in less than a week. Dede Harvey, an ex-minister and a square resident was suddenly the new headmaster, while Al Bauman was promoted to the position of Director of Education in the Synanon Foundation.

I tried to fit in, but didn't have Sister Mary's ability to suspend judgments. Nor Ginnie Schronn's total involvement. When this young schoolteacher from Brandeis moved in for the summer, she was given a lovely room overlooking the ocean. Then, one day, she packed up everything and moved over to one of the girls' dormitories at the Clump. When I asked why, Ginnie answered, "I've come to Synanon to be a part of its life-style. Living in a 'special way' isn't Synanon—I just want to be one of the folks." Drug addicts—folks? I thought she was crazy.

Nor did I have Father Mike's ability to roll with the punches. Another summer resident, he was a diocesan priest from New York, the younger brother of Ted Dibble, a resident ex-addict. Mike's training was in counseling and dramatics; when he arrived at the School, Al Bauman decided he should be a demonstrator in computer science but then changed his mind; so all summer Mike uncomplainingly taught the theories of Buckminster Fuller to the seven-to-fourteen-year-old group.

My only solace at that time was Mary. At first we had a very nice room together in an apartment with two other girls, Fran and Ann. The day after we arrived, Mary had to return to her convent for a going-away party for a priest. When she came back late that night with two uninitiated nuns, she almost fell across a mop of a boy curled on the sofa. Oblivious, I slept on in our room. The nuns gasped, "Who is he, Mary?" She just smiled, "I don't know." The nuns went away amazed that we could put up with it, and Mary woke me up laughing. We prayed together, as we often did in the beginning. Then someone decided we were too tight and not joining in enough, and I was to room with two girls I have never seen before, Roberta and Nancy, in a recently acquired, thoroughly filthy apartment. After spending the day swearing at sponges and ajax, I picked up a copy of *National Geographic,* an issue with a story on Bobby Kennedy's mountain-climbing expedition. I was so exhausted that, seeing the picture of Bobby hugging James Whittiker as they reached the peak for the first time, suddenly had me in tears, mourning his senseless death.

Still sobbing, I heard a knock at the door.

"Hi, Barbara!"

My hands smeared across my eyes. "Hi!" I said.

"My name's Bebe. I hear you're going to share an apartment with me."

"Oh," I tried to smile. "Are you moving in here?"

"Oh no, we're both moving above the Nursery. Roberta will room with you."

"What?" I tried not to yell. "But I've already moved TWICE."

"Oh, well, don't let it get you down. It's just Synanon. You're getting an inside view. Tomorrow's a holiday, we're moving then."

She slammed the screen door.

This is too much, I fumed. They can have their WAM, their kids, their games. I'm sick of being treated like an addict! First they split us up, then they carve me in two. Why didn't I go to summer school like last summer? I wrote such nice poems, and there were regular meals. And all I had to do was vacuum my room!

Later, sitting in Mary's living room on the low sofa, watching the freeway, I cried again. Mary sat before me, her hair newly cropped as her demonstration for Synanon.

"Barbara," she said quietly, "I'm not going to Mass with you anymore."

"Why, Mary?"

"Because I can't bear the sleepy tired way it's offered at St. Anne's. I can't even understand the priest reading the Gospel. There's no participation, nothing—just dead people waiting, far away from a dead altar."

"The altar's not dead, Mary. And it's not Christ's fault."

"I know, Barbara. But I can receive Christ in other ways. Last night, I had the best talk with Mannie. After we were finished, he looked at me and said, 'I think we've just received communion.' And, Barbara, he was right."

What's wrong with me?, I thought. Why don't I have this verbal communion with ex-addicts? "But Mary," I cried, "I need your support."

"You'll always have my support, Barbara. And I'll go to Mass occasionally, when I can really prepare myself. I just hate to have it as a routine; a thing I must perform, like setting my hair."

"That's a horrible way of putting it, Mary. And how will I even get up without you?"

"You'll go it alone, Barbara."

"I have done it before, Mary, before I entered, but I'll miss you. Hey, let's splurge tonight; I'll treat you to a chocolate sundae, a coke, french fries—jelly doughnut?"

She laughed. "Sure, Barb."

Later, I let my body fall from me, and prayed—

> for are we not like the Pharisees who came to Jesus in a body
> and demanded,
> "perform a miracle for us
> to show God's approval"?

In other words, let us not suffer. Let us see, but not feel. Let us hear, but not move. Let us speak, but not pray. Let us find answers without waiting. A miracle, Lord; give us the fullness of life without death.

And as he heard their request, "Jesus gave a deep groan and said:

> why do the people of this day
> ask for a miracle?
> No, I tell you!
> No such proof will be given this people!"

and "With this, he left them" (Mark 8:13, Philips trans.).

# Apprentice Apollo

"No," I mumble. "No. No."

It is a few days later, and I'm sitting among the Mamas' and Papas' tribe.

"No," I begin again.

"Well, asshole, why not?" one of the group asks. "Why don't you like Synanon?"

"At loss for words, child?" Al Bauman smiles.

I want to answer with a well-placed "fuck-you," but can't get it past my voice box. A string snaps. "Well," I begin. Sigh. "It isn't that I don't like it. It's got possibilities and it really does help people. But why in the hell (They grab their seats in laughter. "Tut! Such language," someone screams.) do I need it? I'm young and I'm not a label peeler or a pill popper. I don't want to be told every move I make. Even the convent's freer than this place! And everything's changing so often, there's never time to be free."

"You are the proudest motherfucker! What's so free about your life? Living on a line, answering bells, wearing a zoot suit," one man yells.

"Oh hell. Don't you people ever read a newspaper? I wouldn't even be at Synanon if it hadn't changed. I have more freedom in the convent than I'll ever have here."

"Oh yeah? Can you fuck?"

"No," I answer. "I've chosen not to."

"Why? Afraid?"

"No," I mumble. "I, I—I've made a vow to Christ."

"Jesus Christ! I can't believe in a religion that takes away your womanhood." Twenty heads nod in agreement.

"No," I retort, "that's not right. I don't have to get married to be a woman. I can give my love in other ways."

"Oh? Are you a homosexual?"

"No."

"Who ever said anything about marriage, anyway? Isn't this getting interesting? Tell us, *Sister* Barbara, how you give your love."

"I have my work. Teaching is a way of giving life. Many times my hand on a face, my smile, can help a child. I sense that I have the ability to bring joy. I meet so many people each day. Perhaps, I can love by giving joy, peace—"

"Shut up, ass," Al yells.

"But why, Barbara—why be a virgin?" Midge speaks quietly.

"Damn it! What can I say? Virginity is not an evil, it's—a gift. It's something you make—like bread. Bread takes a long time to produce. Life and love kneads and folds it, lifts and pushes it, into its final shape. Perhaps hope is the yeast. And finally, the bread rises, *not unlike a bomb*—"

"I don't understand a word you're saying," an older woman announces with finality.

I look at Al. Something is smiling in him. "Waiting, Barbara. You'll spend your life waiting. But what are you waiting for?"

"Come off it, Al! A Game's not a time to cerebrate."

"But Barbara, who do you discuss your virginity with?"

"I don't know—when I pray, other nuns, priests." Twenty twisted mouths are laughing again.

A tall man yells, "What a meaningful discussion!"

"Why don't you discuss your virginity with a prostitute?" Midge asks.

"Or a housewife?"

"Or a man?" Al says. "Perhaps they can tell you what virginity really means today. Oh, I forgot—you *know* everything, don't you, Barbara?"

"No," I answer. "I don't know much."

"Did it ever occur to you that being a nun, for *you*, is the easy way out?"

"Yeh, what do you endure?" another man asks. It would help if I knew all their names.

"What crisis do *you* have, asshole?" Al asks.

"Yes, Barbara. What fuckin' right do you have to live without sin?"

"I sin," I retort.

"Not everyday, popcorn sins, asshole."

"Yes, Barabara, we mean the sins most of us have to live with—you know, ocean-sins—night-sins," Midge adds.

"No," I mumble. "I just don't know—don't know."

So I make up this song during the rest of the Game—

If I were to faulknerlike trace
my bloodstream would be a bomb,

the surprise comprised in my begin-
ning and etc. peeling labels

before no wonder left at twelve,
half of my guts greened out

in salingerlike coughfields
yielding no roots, black boots

samson hair, the strip
zipper dance, a bomb

solemn harmonicas, being bored
sometimes gored and tracing

the racing moneystream
from faulknerlike bears;

apprentice apollo—
if i knew a myth,

bombing from the bomb
going to the bomb

mostly bombed tracing
trust in the rust

of a key—
if i could find a key.

Then slowly, as if from behind a wall, I hear them attack one of the Mamas and Papas—Betty. It seems she had dared to take a cocktail before she came to the Game.

"But it was hours ago. My son and his wife came all the way from New York!"

"Stop bullshitting, Betty. You know the rules. It must have been more than one for Jerry to smell you."

I lean forward. *"You're the biggest hypocrite, Betty."* I space my words carefully. "You're just like all parents—do what I tell, not what I do down deep." I'm yelling.

Betty has strong eyes. "What right—what right do you have to say that to me, you little bitch!"

I, too, have strong eyes. "No right! Only that you're a hypocrite, that's all!"

Later, walking, I ask myself: Which is more Christian? To lose and be lost and be found quietly in God—or to be me—running, taking what I can, giving out of guilt and grief?

I remember a few days previous, when Sister Mary and I visited my parents' home.

My Dad offers us a drink. I look at Mary, remembering those two rules—

no violence allowed (verbal violence welcomed)

no chemicals, drugs, or alcohol permitted (for a resident, no drinks at any time; for a square Game player, no drinks prior to coming to Synanon)

We don't bother to explain. Quietly, Mary asks for a coke. I take the vodka, making freedom an excuse, figuring time and gum will make me fine before returning. There is no comment from Mary, not even a gesture.

My mother asks, "Barbara, why do you and Mary insist on being exorcists? First, the convent, and now Synanon, of all places. Why can't you two be normal, get a job, marry, vote, pay taxes?"

I want to drop a lug on her. I want to shut her up. I want to tell her that there is blood smeared everywhere and my generation knows it. We feel the sin of our times, whatever it is; some of us become violent; others let peace explode within them. I know what it is to thrash about, to be a cornered animal. All we've got is a life of movement: "Let us run, until we arrive" (St. Augustine): gotta go, gotta catch, gotta me.

My mother waits. "Isn't a family enough for you, Mary?"

"Of course it is, Mrs. Austin. But right now, Barbara and I feel a deeper dedication to life—and to healing." She sips her coke.

"But you've got to have time for yourself. You can't just give and give. You'll give away yourself, Mary," my mother sips.

"Don't worry, Mom," I answer. "Mary and I know how to keep some for ourselves—We know when to stop." A chorus of sips.

Mother faces me. "You'll always know when to stop, Barbara. I've *never* worried about that ability. You haven't changed a bit, nun or no nun. *You'll* always take enough for yourself. Have you written your poor Aunt Sarah yet?"

"No," I answer.

So. I am Eleanor's daughter. Hypocrite yelling hypocrite—it is an old human gap, we give it new names. So many crutches, so many hangups—and I don't have any?

What right do I have to be free of the ocean-sins, the night-sins?

> If God takes care of the birds of the air
> He will feed them in a cage (St. Augustine).

There is a story told of Apollo's son. He was not satisfied with his human power. He asked to fly with God. The god said no many times, but finally, worn smooth, he mumbled yes. His son pulled the heavy reins tight, the horse's nostrils whitened with the pain, the preparation: gotta go, gotta catch, gotta me.

# Dan the collector man

Then I met Dan Marsh. He told me, "Caged rats run the rim of their cage, I ran the rim of my mind." He smiled a little, and I watched his heavy eyelashes.

He was sitting in back of a low table in his tribe room, "The Oversoul." Synanon seems to have a fear of regular-size desks—probably from sitting in front of too many police, hospital, psychiatrist, and parole officers' desks.

He fingered a few pieces of colored glass. His table contained some linoleum with holes punched in it to hold incense, a silver pistol cigarette lighter, an orange letter holder, a mosaic letter opener, an old car horn, a twisted flute, a trombone with its air slide gone. In fact, Dan's whole room was a museum. On the wall beside him hung a faded, yellow picture of his father, a man with red hair. Near it was a psychedelic view of the "Oversoul," the transcendental name for the deity. Books were stacked up behind him, mostly Emerson and Thoreau, but with some Hemingway and Faulkner. Everything from the bright green and blue ash tray to the magazines was on display. Gingerly, I picked up a few of the items, fearful that the museum attendant might catch me.

Dan had light red hair and the sort of complexion that fades into the white shirt he always seemed to be wearing. Tall, responsible, and a fine speaker, he was in charge of the Cloverfield Clump, besides being tribe leader.

"Hey Tim, did you get your room cleaned up?" Dan looked at a man in a thin T-shirt.

"Yeh. I'm sorry it was such a mess."

A Mexican boy leaned forward. "You're lucky. One time Dan turned over every damn bed in the dorm." Laughter.

Dan picked up some incense. His hands had such a sensuous delight in things, one could tell he knew all about something just by its touch. "You're lucky, Juan! When I was over in one of the old Venice dorms, my tribe leader took all my clothes out of the closet and piled them smack in the center of the room. I walked over them and occasionally around them for three days, cursing my roommate before I realized they were mine."

"How'd you ever get to Synanon, Dan?" I wanted to know.

"Easy, Barb. Just try drugs." They were laughing.

"No, I mean it, Dan. What led you here?"

"Caged rats run the rim of the cage, I ran the rim of my mind," he smiled again.

"Poetry?" I said.

"Disordered, dingbat mind poetry, Barbara. I was just a hard core dope fiend, that's all. Irresponsible, all the hangups. I was going to be a doctor once but quit college when taking drugs became more fun than studying them. Began the whole delicious, third world route. My friends called me Dirty Red." He laughed.

"How long have you been here?" asked Ginnie, the square who taught with me at the school.

"You mean altogether?"

"Huh?" I didn't understand.

"I was here for two years, then went wild, broke into Medical and stole some drugs and took off . . . I've been back now about two years." Dan picked up a delicate watch that was lying on a cork mat.

"But what happened here to change you? You've got one of the most important jobs in the Foundation, besides taking care of the sixty people in your tribe."

"Seventy-five people, Barb. Seventy-six with Ginnie, here. Let's put it this way. You spend the long night netting nothing. You've got brains, perhaps talent, at least your own particular beauty, but you're always catching nothing or having traffic accidents. You wreck your medical career, ostracize your family, are divorced by your wife, steal, lie, cheat, maybe even kill."

I gulped and looked at Ginnie. "Kill?"

"In Mexico. An accident." He never said anything more about it, but leaned forward on his chair and told us how they put him in a tortilla prison. There he was, lying on the Mexican dirt with the cockroaches doing the "la cucaracha" all over him. He tried to wrap himself in his magnificent cardboard bedding but it was so ridiculous he gave up. During hot days and cold nights, he lay in a Mexican-style cardboard coffin, dreaming he was a cactus. Alone and magnificent, in the center of the desert, with his arms spread out and 10,000 heroin needles sticking in his body.

On Sundays he'd smell flowers slowly opening on the cactus. It would be visiting day for those who had pesos. He'd lean his greasy red hair on the thick bars, smelling the food and hearing the staccato talk. Then he'd get sick again, and the beans and his loneliness would run out together.

But he endured. He learned endless variations of Spanish obscenities and he wrote letters to himself on the dirt floor, which the cockroaches quickly covered with their wild dance. Yet he couldn't contain his desire to create. If he could not make a decent bed out of his cardboard coffin, at least he could make himself some eating utensils. He stole a tin bean can and worked endlessly to shape it into a fairly smooth plate. Hour after hour, he'd rub and beat it against his jail bars. His hands bled at first but even the bleeding was good. Then he made a fork for himself. A sense of completion as he held his work up to the sun. Then, one night, they came for him; put their hands on his dirt-hardened clothes and dragged him away from his tin masterpeices. They should show a little respect, I'm a beaner now, he thought. In the back of a pickup, he did not ask where he was going: all he knew was that it was good to be lying on metal again. The truck coughed and finally began to move. Well, I'm going to die; Dirty Red is dead, he thought to himself. From the truck lights all he could make out was sagebrush; he considered the possibility of jumping, and dreamt of living off the land, catching rabbits with his bare hands, drinking juice from a cactus. Then the desert began to pursue him, its grainy hands outstretched, and he woke up to a warm day in a small town. The sheriff was looking him over carefully, and Dan began to lie for every bean he had eaten in jail. "I'm a poor American who came to Mexico for a visit and was wrongly accused of a crime in a barroom brawl. Give me the fare to Arizona and I'll never come back." He didn't know if they believed him, but felt they didn't want an American in the prison any longer. They gave him the money. He stood in the shower for two hours before two-thirds of the grime and the dead cockroaches would come off and then he was free.

"So I took the bus to Arizona. Lied some more when I got

there, tried to go straight, failed—tried, failed, ad nauseam." He got up, laughed again, and showed us the apartment he and his wife June had recently been given. She also had a very responsible job as head of Finance at the Club. They had moved into the back part to leave the kitchen, dining room, and sitting room for the girls in the Clump to use as a sewing center, called the Beehive.

"Well, we talk a lot about containment. So June and I decided when we moved here to practice a little." He pointed to a medium-size chest on the floor, and told us how he discovered it. He was walking in the warehouse one day at Synanon's San Francisco facility (called the Seawall) inspecting a new shipment of castoffs that different benefactors had sent. Over in the corner, half under a chair and supporting two cushions, was a filthy chest. Suddenly, Dan said, he remembered Mexico. He knelt down and rubbed a spot clean: it was golden brown underneath, and the carving was deep. When he took it home, June and he began working. For awhile it was their child; they rubbed and washed it until, at last, it throbbed beneath their hands.

Synanon had brought out the art in Dan. Yes, he had known it vaguely before when he studied, in brief moments when he loved, and when he rubbed the tin bean can into a silver fire, but now he understood that the time one spent rubbing darkness away was worth it. The hours spent in the Games, listening to Chuck's tapes, working and struggling to understand his darkness, and that of others, was worth it.

Of course, Synanon had been the artist, because it believed in man creating man. And now it had taught Dan what Dionysius the Areopagite had written long ago about "the darkness beyond being":

> For this is like the art of those who carve a natural image from stone, removing from around it all that prevents the pure vision of the veiled form, revealing its hidden beauty solely by taking away.

The second time Dan returned to Synanon, he crawled all the way home. All he had in his pocket was a wrinkled picture of a proud, swarthy man who looked like Genghis Khan. This time Synanon began to work upon him with its non-violent life and its violent verbal existence. It squeezed and clubbed him until he was a toilet. Flush it, baby, flush it! Until no trace is left—until, of course, the next time and the next. He began, finally, to take away the darkness himself. Until he was golden and smooth inside, like the chest on his living room rug. But still imperfect, like the chest with its painful crack right down the center of its side.

A few days after Dan showed us the Clump, I sat in on an executive Game listening to the others jump on him.

"Why in the hell do you have two offices, Dan? Can't you be like everyone else and make your tribe room your office?"

"You preach containment, baby, but you don't practice it."

Dan smiled. "I like my tribe room to be a place where we can relax. And I need another office for business at the Clump."

"You are the biggest fuckin' scavenger around. Watch out, everybody. Dan gets up at 1 A.M. to get to the warehouse before us."

"Yeah, Dan," Ron said. "I couldn't find a fuckin' chair for my fuckin' tribe room because you had them all!"

"Okay, Ron. Fine. Come down and take one. Take two," Dan said.

I wanted to stick up for Dan. After all, he was living in one-third of what all of them had because of his generosity about the Beehive. But you do not protect another in a Game, you let them grow by taking it. Besides, my words would only have backfired.

"Hey, Dan, there's something more important I want to indict you with," Ron began again.

"Shoot."

"Why in hell don't you send Eddy some cigarettes?"

"What?" Rick yelled. "You mean you've got a poor dingbat at Camarillo Mental Hospital and you don't even bother to send him cigs?"

"He's too busy stealing chairs!" Ron inserted.

*"Wait a minute."* Dan was angry now. "I've talked to the doctor and he says Ed's not cooperating up there at all. So, until he does, and I've told him this too, *personally,* no WAM and no cigarettes."

"Since when, Dan Marsh, you cocksucker, have we ever listened to doctors? Since when have they ever helped one fuckin' bit? It's the doctors who say addicts are incurable; since when have we listened?"

"And besides, you proud chair-stealing motherfucker, this guy is nuts. I mean he blew his lid. How can he understand your asshole punishment? What shitty good'll it be to take the one thing he enjoys except salve your fuckin' hostilities?"

"I felt this would show him we meant business," Dan answered.

"You bullshitting asshole! Didn't we promise, don't we promise every dingbat who comes in here that Synanon will take care of them, lock, stock, and barrel—disordered guns that they are?"

How easy it is to forget, I thought. Here Dan had stolen from Synanon, yet Synanon had taken him back, let him marry June, accepted his two children from another marriage, and even put him in charge of a tribe. And now he wouldn't give nutty-Eddy some cigarettes!

Aloud, I said, "It seems to me that you're letting your work turn into another Institution, Dan. The Church, the Government, does no better. Give it to him if he is good, punish the sucker if he's naughty."

Dan looked down. "I didn't see it that way. I gave him WAM and cigarettes at first, but he wasn't trying up there. But maybe you're right. I guess I was too tough on the poor nut." Unless we become like little children—apparently Dan had forgotten that Synanon's power will always be in its weakness. And what about the power of the Church, I wondered; if only we could play a few Synanon Games in the convent!

On the wall in Dan's living room is the framed picture of the swarthy man who was once proud and tough, a wrinkled Genghis Khan, the picture he carried wherever he went for eleven years. Like the golden chest, it has a prominent place in his new living room. It is a memory, the other is a testament.

And I was a fool, coming to Synanon thinking I could collect interesting stories for my students. I've even mistitled this chapter. Dan is a man. And because he is a man, he is too busy giving and grieving to waste his time collecting and labeling life.

# *Part of Synanon's brood*

I am living inside of an egg. My mind is a yolk sac. Nothing to do, sitting alone by a cheap table outside of Synanon's dining room, my glasses hanging from one ear. Is this withdrawal? Am I some mind addict who has to shuck it all and meet Synanon at last? Won't someone come to this table? What's wrong with me? I remember what Al Bauman said to me in a Mamas' and Papas' Game: "Dowdy-Barbara. Why don't you find some other color besides blue?" He doesn't know how I've tried to get used to these light clothes.

Last night I dreamt that it was Sunday—must get to Mass. The time ticked fearfully by. Finally we leave, but instead of going to Church we end up at a diner. I am not brave enough to say that I don't want to eat, so I follow them in. Waiting, waiting, then blurting out miserably, "I have to go to Church." They laugh at me. I don't remember who I was with, except that there are two men, one rather heavy. He keeps making fun of me. So, finally I say,

"Do you know what you are?"

He gives me a half-cocked smile and says, "What?"

"A Big Penis," I tell him.

The rats of the day are crawling in me as I enter the spacious dining room. Deliberately, I sit by a group of people I don't know. In typical Synanon fashion everybody is introduced, and we begin to eat the salad.

"How long were you in the Army, Mabel?" they ask the huge girl who is sitting next to me.

"Four years, ten days, five hours, thirty-six minutes, and two seconds."

We laugh. "Did you like it?"

"Hated every dirty minute of it."

"Then why did you stay four years, nine days, etc.?"

"The money and the drugs, baby."

"You began there?"

"Yep." She humps over her food, an escapee from an L.A. roller rink. "Began and ended. The stuff is easy to get."

Dinner is finally over, and I strain forward, looking for someone I know. There's Mel, the black who was so kind to us the very first night Mary and I waddled in with our great black habits. He puts his strong arms around me.

"Hi, Barb. How's it goin'?"

"Bad, Mel. I'm going on a Trip Friday and I'm scared to death. Tonight's my pre-Trip Game."

We sit down at a table outside the dining room from where we can see the huge, sunken ballroom. Usually a lot of people mill around after dinner, then it fades out during Game time (8 P.M.) and gets crowded when Games let out around ten-thirty. It is only five-thirty now. Within ten minutes there're four or five other people sitting with us, and I'm introduced to a handsome gray-haired Italian called Saba.

"Have you ever gone on a Trip before, Barbara?"

"No. Why do they have a pre-Trip Game if everything is supposed to happen during the forty-eight-hour period?"

"It introduces you to the people and lets you know their problems. It will probably last longer than most Games you've been in. It'll get you so uptight that you'll burst open on the Trip . . . At first you'll hate them all, Barbara, then you'll love them.

"What was your Trip like, Saba?"

"It was the most beautiful human experience I've ever had. I live in Beverly Hills and come to Synanon a few times a week for the Games, the spa, and the sea. But I wanted a deeper experience of the life here, so I signed up for a Trip."

"But what do you do on it?"

"I can't explain it to you. You have to go through it yourself. We all had to wear the same tan tunic and sandles. You can't wear any makeup or jewelry. But, of course, that won't worry you, Sister. You'll spend at least sixteen hours in Games. And for the rest, it will depend on what kind of activities Ted Dibble, your Trip Leader, decides to do.

"Activities?"

"Yes. Music, dancing, Games—things like that."

"Now let me get this straight. I go into the Game Friday

night at seven and it's over at eight Sunday night. Forty-eight hours—weren't you exhausted?"

"No. Exhilarated's the word. If you want, you can sleep for a few hours each day but it's better to keep going the whole while, trying to be utterly open, listening, working hard in the Games. A few people remain closed and miss the Trip. But it's always only a few, I'm told."

Mel touches me. "Yeh, the Trip really works, Barbara."

"Just try like hell to be open, go along with whatever is asked of you, and you'll have a great Trip. I did. On Sunday night after we came down, I—"

"What do you mean, 'came down'?"

"Haven't you ever seen people come off a Trip?"

"No."

"Well, the whole Trip is up on the next floor. You use that long Stew room for all your general meetings with Ted Dibble and the smaller rooms for your Games. There's usually fifty people to a Trip and they're broken down to groups of twelve or so for the Games. On Sunday night, every Club member waits around the ballroom to see those fifty joyful people run downstairs. They play the Hoopla and everyone joins in. It's marvelous.

"Sounds that way," I sigh.

"You know, Barbara, after my Trip, I was so happy that I went and worked a whole day even though I hadn't slept for three. My secretary, my wife, my men, couldn't believe my joy. Don't be afraid, it'll be the best thing for you."

Mel was smiling at me. "What sign are you, Barbara."

"Oh, I'm not much for astrology, Mel."

"But what are you, Barb?" he persists.

I am embarrassed. "A Virgo."

Two or three laugh. "*Too* much!" Someone says.

Mel explains that he is a Scorpio, and warns me that the spider, scorpion, has to be approached with the utmost gentleness or it will strike out. The thing to do is to sneak up on it from its back and grab it quickly around its hard plastic middle, between its two sets of legs. A Scorpio person, he says, cannot be approached straightforwardly; do that and you're dead. But come quietly from the back, and they'll go gentle in your hands.

His mind turns back to a time when he was a forest ranger in Oregon. It is summer, he tells us, and huge drops of sweat are congregating on his neck, so he sits down on an old corroded log. The great sun is making him dizzy and he can smell the heat rising from the brittle ground. Suddenly he hears something move by his feet. Bending his head, he sees an enormous scorpion as big as his fist. Suddenly he sees two scorpions; they are both hopping, and now he's hopping too. They hop a little and he hops a little.

I stare at Mel. Somebody at the table says, "Like hell, Mel." And Mel looks up with his blacksheepish, holding-the-trump card grin, and says, "As sure as I'm sitting by a nun at Synanon, it's true."

I can't stand it anymore. My Game is at 8:30 P.M. It's early; most people are at the main dinner, and the side area of the first floor is very quiet. The new residents who are trying to kick the habit live here the first few days that they're at Synanon. Further away, a small circle of easy chairs stands by a huge reading table, but tonight, I can't sit still with a book. I walk by the long sofas where the addicts lie during their withdrawal. Synanon believes they shouldn't be alone during their drug-leaving time, so people watch beside them day and night. Unlike standard procedure in the County places, the addicts are not shoved into some square hospital room. Rather, they are put near enough to people so that their pain and loneliness can take the objective form of hope expressed in *The Synanon Philosophy:* "The power which resides in [man] is new in nature, and none but he knows what it is that he can do nor does he know until he has tried."

A man who has been alone with his weakness for years finds it very hard to leap beyond his present difficult situation. But when he can watch others who have broken out, and who now can talk, laugh, play cards, read, dance around him, perhaps he can believe, "Yeh, yeh—I've got a chance. I can be ex-bad man, made new in nature!"

I let my hand trail along the sofa in the silence. The sofa is deep, the windows high, but tonight I can't see my beloved self-renewing ocean. Just a few palm trees and the clouds. But there's been so much of Mel, penises, scorpions, Saba, the Trip,

I can't silence myself enough to watch the clouds—it seems an infinite task to watch them. Then suddenly, I see a small plane traveling upward through them; by keeping my eyes fixed on it, I can turn again to the clouds. I feel their movement; for a moment, there is a free-from-body joy.

This environment is doing something to me. First, I can't pray. Now, it's a super-effort to watch clouds fold and unfold. What is happening to me? Where are they taking me?

# The volcanic orange

Go and call in the last dregs of the city. Lift a bus from a scummy street, unhitch one passenger train from its filthy tracks, steal four cars from a swift, cold freeway, dump their contents on Synanon. Play God with people. Believe that dirty words become flesh when people sit together in a rectangular, immobile room; that thirteen needy men and women can become love-apostles if they are forced to sit quietly enough to yell at each other. So, seat them in a circle around a central fire. Internalize the fire. Close the door. Begin.

I fasten my seat belt, surrounded by a collage of people. The only familiar face is that self-styled, walking brain, John Barry, who came to Synanon a M.D. alcoholic and now teaches anatomy next door to me at the Synanon School. The small shreds of my novitiate training in mortification are a help with John; he is such a bore. I want to stick out my sharp red tongue at that small pock-marked face that epitomizes everything the brain cannot do.

For the next few hours, however, we are going to try the emotions. We begin on mini-James, the mustachioed homosexual who seems to gloat over his little yellow story.

He tells us he had to prove himself a man, so he finds a pretty nineteen-year-old college sophomore, and lives with her in the small pool of sex and love games.

"So what's wrong with that?" they ask.

His little apple flops up and down. "Well, I cheated on her five times."

"With guys or girls?"

He doesn't look at me. "Guys," he says.

The way he uses his stubby fingers to count the times is disgusting. We feel in our guts that he's only a little talk-and-pity engine. Toot. Toot. Jamie-Peanut-Butter.

"Shut up, Jim, you cocksucker," Mike, our Game leader says. I had heard about Mike. He was not an addict but had come to Synanon because he wanted to do something with his life. He had been a P.R. man for some movie company, but at twenty-three all the green dollars were dust for him, and for three years now he had let Synanon get under his skin. The young, Jewish intellectual look—heavy beard, stooped shoulders, even the thick reading glasses—reminded me of a guy I had dated in high school, all mouth. Why did he speak that language all during the Game? Couldn't he say anything without punctuating it with fuck, cock, or asshole?

A pre-Trip Game is like playing with a volcano. I only played volcanoes once before; while student-teaching at a parish school we studied volcanic eruptions in science class. I got a huge orange and pricked one small hole in it with a pin. After using every bit of my body-pressure to force its rich juice out, I said that this is how much earth pressure it takes to force lava out, and this is vaguely how a volcanic eruption is in relation to our earth. Now we sit and prick thirteen-minute holes in a great orange world; will we use our word knives to do a cross section on the orange?

We turn to Maureen, a rather bloated gray-haired woman of sixty-five with a good, sad heart. "Just call me Mo," she giggles. "I work part time for Welfare." She's the kind of woman who lets others go first, and when she finally gets there, finds the toilet roll empty.

I watch the silver hair on her face.

"Why in the hell's an old woman going on a Trip?"

"Yeah, can you make it, lady? Isn't sixty-five too old to go to the moon?"

She smiles. "Look, Sonny, I may be older than you, but there's strong guts under this fat!"

She begins to run her story. How she recently remarried after her husband of twenty years died. Oh yes, and this seems an afterthought, long, long ago when America was in the deep pit of the Depression, she married a Negro. It was in Detroit and black Sam owned a bar and she loved him for a while. She started to go into other things but I had to interrupt. Even my idle reading of Baldwin, Cleaver, and James Wright made me believe that her talk was as false as her teeth.

"Do you mean to tell me," I growled, "that this Negro is only a little stain in your life? That you have no personal regrets, old woman, about divorcing him—no guilt?"

She bobs her old head, "Well, it just didn't work out—

Besides, it's almost twenty-five years ago. And I felt so sorry for the children."

"You have children by him?"

"Oh, yes. They're both mulatto. One is quite dark, the other is lighter. One married a black man; the other never married."

"You must have a lot more hidden under that fat, Mo. You mean to tell us that this marriage is something you've simply cancelled out? As if it never really happened?"

"Well," Mo began.

"But don't you see it," Mike yells at her, "smell it, feel it in the fucking pain of your children?"

"Yes. Yes. I suppose."

"Yes, yes, I suppose, she says. Good God!"

But all we could do now is prick the orange and apply a minimum of word-pressure. This old woman, all these years trying to grease herself clean with nice, white crisco. What must it do to her to look at her checkerboard children?

*"Shit!"*

It was all so easy in the convent. When people got you down, you could go into your cell, and pull the world in behind you. *Your* world, not this acrimonious box, this sardine can stuffed with people's sins. Take Dorothy. She is deliberately making herself pathetic to pull me apart. I don't want to hear about your thirty years of shame as a muscular dystrophy cripple. Do you hear that, Dorothy? I don't want to notice how you edged up the stairs to our pre-Trip room, one laborious step at a time. I don't want to remember how they offered to carry you and you refused. Why this hardjawed pride, Dorothy? Why this clinging to your trembling courage? Now she is telling us how she has had six affairs to prove herself. Some girl about my age yells,

"I don't believe it!"

"What do you mean?" Dorothy looks scared.

"I can't believe a man would crawl into bed with you!"

I can't look at her. Why does life here always zero down to sex? Isn't there any other way to become yourself?

There are three groups of people at Synanon. The full-time residents like Mike, John, a short-haired young girl, and Sean, a young guy from New York; the non-resident Game players and the parents of Synanon residents. Joan is such a parent. Her daughter is twenty-four and at a Synanon facility in San Diego.

Someone asks Joan if she feels any resentment toward her daughter for all the trouble she has caused her. She blinks, shakes her head. "No. I love her, I forgive her." But they keep pricking that orange. "Are you sure?" "What's the worse thing you've ever done?"

She starts crying. "The worst thing, the worst thing," she keeps saying. I watch the people smother their cigarettes as if those dirty white sticks were her. Isn't this ever going to end? Who will put the bus back on the dirty street, rehitch the train, gently set the cars back on tomorrow's freeway? Who will play God and heal us? Why must we go on squeezing the sore pimple of men's souls?

Mike is yelling, "Tell it, Joan. Be a big girl, *tell it*—"

"Once I was so tired, so tired," she sniffles. One night her daughter has taken an overdose of her joy-pills and is slowly smothering to death on the smooth, warm sofa. Joan comes in and stands over her, transformed with power. She could let her die and all this pain would be ended. She would be free at last from this spoiled brat. And she sits down. For a long moment Joan gets ready to sit and watch her daughter crumple into dust. Then her voice catches like a child's and in a moment she is crying again, My only child, my little girl—"

"Stop your fucking sniffling, Joan," Mike orders; then, although he knows the answer: "Are you divorced?"

"Yes, I'm divorced."

"You can't do much with your life or your child, can you? I suppose you've followed thc usual path . . . Have any affairs lately?" She looks up. There are a thousand holes in her Kleencx. "Yes, I have," she says quietly and firmly. "Six months ago, I guess."

"You guess: so sheepish, big bone, I mean Joan. Was he married?"

A hesitation. "Yes."

He looks around the room. "Did you hear that, folks? This female cocksucker wants to let her kid die because her kid's so damn evil."

"I didn't say she was evil! I said I was tired," Joan is screaming.

It's so damn futile. We're all riddled. I looked at Mike with hatred; leave her alone, my eyes bark.

"Sister?"

I blanch. All that I am at that moment takes refuge in my eyes. I am Joan's child, let me die.

"Isn't there something in Catholic teaching about a woman like this?"

'What do you mean?"

"A commandment about love of children and faithfulness. Is adultery a sin, Sister?"

"Yes. You know that."

"Is she a sinner?"

"I don't know," I murmur. It was a lie, out of fear, but any other answer seemed worse.

"What do you mean? You don't know?"

"I can't judge her."

Everybody is laughing . . . Someone says, "The Church has judged for two-thousand years." There is nothing to say. I look at Joan. Like me, she is a hopping scorpion.

Suddenly we are looking at the young, cold girl in the corner, I learn her name, Fran, but don't understand how such a smooth face can already have a web of wrinkles around the mouth. She seems to dance before my eyes. Awkward yet mature, one moment she is younger than twenty-two; the next, much older. What she has in common with me, I'm not yet sure. But, not only is she me, she is Mo and her sad heart; she is Dorothy and her dying limbs. And surely, she is a part of Joan, living somewhere down in the San Diego of her soul.

They are cutting into her with their can-opener mouths. Slowly, she spills out. Until nine months ago she was an addict and a prostitute. At sixteen, she had her first affair; by nineteen she was living with a guy in San Francisco. Then one foggy day, the golden bridge of her childhood falls down. She meets and falls in love with a pimp who starts her off on the red light beat. "Of course," she says, "I was high class."

"Did you ever take a dollar?"

"No. Even when I had left him and was on my own, I never charged less than ten dollars."

Mike looks around the stale room. "Well, Fran. You're

about the youngest person here, next to Sean. Yet, you've gone through much more than all of us. Why didn't you say something when we were on Joan? Why didn't you help out in the Game when we needed your knowledge?"

"Don't make me laugh, Mike. What do I have to give?" The wrinkles tighten around Fran's mouth.

"A lot, Fran. You'll soon find out. Why did you keep your asshole mouth shut?"

"I said things, Mike. I said something to Dorothy."

"One person's not enough in a Game, you know that. In your nine months here, you've played at least a thousand Games. Why don't you share yourself, you fuckin' female asshole! Instead, you sit for three hours gloating."

"Who's gloating? You have no fuckin' right, Mike."

"As long as I am Game leader in this room, I have every right . . . Now pick someone to get!"

She is looking frantically around the room. It is late, we must have spent at least an hour on Joan. And there is some horrible guy across the room with a thin mustache and a goatee, named Kent. He's leaning back on his chair, looking at me through sex-sneering eyes. I'm so tired. I don't want to go on this damn Trip. These people are so screwed up, so damn immature . . . I'd like to—

"Who are you?" Fran is looking at me.

I jerk. "My name's Barbara Austin—and you're not the youngest girl in this room. I'm twenty-two."

She laughs. "Twenty-two! I don't believe it. I thought you were at least thirty!"

"Why didn't you call yourself Sister Barbara?" Mike shouts.

"Because I am sick and tired of being used as a punching bag by people who've got a grudge against the Church. I want to be Barbara during this Trip, if you'll let me."

"Who's stopping you, asshole? If you're ashamed that you're a nun, that's your own fault."

"I'm not ashamed. I'm just sick of people thinking I have sex problems."

"Remember, nun, you said it. Not us."

"I've been in enough Games, Mike, to know what people are thinking. Everything in this hole comes down to sex or drugs."

"Whew," James exclaims. "You'll be hard to crack."

"Why'd you come to this Trip, anyway?" Fran yells.

"I don't know. I really don't."

"Maybe it's because you want to learn the truth," Sean says.

"Why wouldn't you tell Joan the truth about herself?" Mike asks.

"I couldn't. I don't know what's happening inside of her. And neither do you."

Mike is furious. "Oh. Would you like to run this Game?"

"Not particularly. But no one can say anything unless you stop running your mouth."

He stares at me, then responds gently, "All right, I'll shut up."

"It's no use talking to her," John says contemptuously. "Besides, her Institution is crumbling anyway. But there's one thing they *do* teach in the Catholic Church—"

I know John is an ex-Catholic. "What's that, John?" I ask.

"How to argue while the world is caving in."

"Like hell, it's caving in," I answer.

Suddenly the top part of the only window in the room falls closed. Everybody is startled and we begin to laugh. Sean falls on his knees in a mock attitude of prayer. "O my God, we're sorry. We didn't mean to call Sister an asshole!"

Mike is laughing too. "It's no use talking to her now folks, even the window's for her! Like brain-child John says, the Church trains its people well."

My body sighs with joy as they turn on Vance, the handsome man next to me. It's time to go, but Mike, as usual, has a few choice words for him. He is thirty-one and very lonely. He says he's not gay, but rarely dates. He is an artist and lives in Manhattan Beach and has come to Synanon to get out of his tight arty life and meet some people. They are getting on him because he hasn't said or added anything to the Game. He tells them he's very tired and didn't have time for dinner before coming, and that his stomach was growling so loud he couldn't hear a lot of what was being said. As they yell at him, I look outside at the night. The old, mossy hotels near the Del Mar are lit, and there, in between them, is the dark sky, the full moon.

Finally, the Game is over. I turn to Vance and offer him the apple I have in my purse. He gruffly refuses it. As I walk downstairs to the jitney, I laugh at myself. Perhaps I am Eve.

*"They beat our rumps to make us breathe"*

—A. MacLeish *J. B.*

It is very easy for me to die. I lie in bed and compose my face, rigor-mortizing myself in the sweet ruts of the sheets, pretending that at last my wide places are filled with the soft stench of flowers and tear-filled people. Slowly, they file past me, staring at my face. One side is completely me, the other is empty. There is no dried blood or skin, but rather, a hollow place, as if half my face is made of steel. Half of me is living, the other is asleep like stone. A small child leans over to kiss the wrong side. His lips become caked with cold. His eyes are dark, his body trembles for many things. He turns to his mother, Bebe, who once shared an apartment with me at Synanon. I try to see her out of my one good eye but she is faceless. All I see is Alex, her son. He and I share the beaten rug near our apartment's one asset, the T.V. Today he is watching one of his Saturday morning cartoons, "Gargantua," and nibbling the cheap hard candy from the Synanon store. I want to see his mother one last time, but there is only Alex. Bebe's whole being circles in her son's dark shyness. It is well that I am dead; I could not support such motherhood.

I try to move my other face. It seems that the enormous sores of the world have festered there, dried, and scraped half of me out. Steel does not twitch. I lie silent, as blond Ginny, who works at the Club switchboard and shares my apartment, steps near. Her teenaged daughter, Linda, sits near me in the children's Stew. Linda's hoarse yelling fills the space between my skin and bones.

"Liar. Bullshitting liar!" she leans across the boy next to her.

"Well, so what? At least my Mom's not a bum."

Did the rest of the children hear his sly rasp? Linda sets her body hard: "She *was* a bum, she's not anymore."

That bleach that Ginny wears like a star on her hair is Synanon; for Synanon is a forgiveness-factory. Take one thousand sins and one thousand Games and bleach your soul clean. After all, sin is but a word. Forgiveness is a person.

Ginny must have been a high-class prostitute. Linda told me that she had had a fountain in her bedroom. I can see her, after my funeral, putting bleach all over our apartment. Setting up fountains of bleach to wash away wherever my poor body's been.

Another child kisses me. Afterward, he licks his lips as if they had touched a dentist's drill. It is my roommate's child David. His pockets are full of an insatiable love for anything that hops, crawls, or slithers. If I strain, yes, he is holding the butterfly I gave him. Mark, his freckled brother, doesn't heed his warning, kisses me, then flutters his hands. I have seen dogs do that with their paws after they've gone to the bathroom by a tree. A vain effort to cover something shameful. Cover the dying side of my face before Tara—Tara, the seven-year-old mulatto queen, now pulling at Roberta her mother. No kiss; words: "What's wrong? What happened to Sither?" And I remember wondering how she ever got such children, one blond-haired, one black-haired, and one just black. Roberta's red hair is a brush at the end of a long, pocked handle, and her words run quickly through the hard space in her thin teeth.

I want to draw an invisible wall between our beds. It worked well when I had to share a room with my younger brother; he had to knock on air to come in to borrow a Kleenex. But I am not made of air; Roberta's talk carries me into a night I do not understand. Having let the wall between us float away, I crawl up and down my bed, refluffing my pillow; I need sleep —but still I listen.

Her life is of peeling marriages, the last one enduring eight days. He was her connection and in trouble. If she testified against him, she'd be another swallow in the Syndicate's dry throat. So she lets her Negro trumpet player husband go and marries a man she loathes.

We sit together in the dark, and Roberta tells me how she and another girl do a nude wrestle for five hundred bucks while some weirdo watches, flashing his eternally petrified snapshot mind. She says her first marriage at sixteen ends abruptly one rainy Christmas Eve, when, after a fight, her husband comes after her with a knife. Finally, he simply locks her out in the rain.

The sky is breaking apart, the wind is blowing the roof down in red pieces, and she sits on the uncovered porch in her bra and panties. The people are coming home from their warm Christmas Eves. Their eyes filmy with liquor, they laugh and stare at this pink Santa Claus bucked from her reindeer. Four hours pass, dumbly she walks home to her parents.

O cold Emmanuel—she arrives at her parents' door without a donkey. They lean against the lock, praying to their Catholic God that this small failure will find some other inn. She leaves their desert, carrying the light luggage of her youth, and stubble of spring in her body, a tight beginning called David.

Another marriage, and she is swallowed up by California. She becomes religious and joins the Pentecostals. For a long time, a lifetime, she lives with this second husband, and Mark awakens in her. The endless drag of mops and T.V., dust and diapers—finally, she drops the laying on of hands and takes up the laying in of a needle. She loses her second man but somehow stumbles through the days because the nights and the needle keep her alive and cool.

She meets a black man with a silver horn, loves him, stays married nine years, builds a throne for Tara, the youngest, and then her connection gets caught. The hollow running begins. For a whole year red-head Roberta lives alone in Oregon, her kids cloistered in foster homes. All she's got is the dirty eyelet pattern of one body, a soul. She is dying when she arrives at Synanon, having lived on candy bars and heroin.

The morning comes too soon after our talks. There is a bed to be made, dust to be cleaned from the corners of our room. What can I give her? Once, I leave a New Testament on her pillow, a gift from the Catholic fairy. Another time, a grandiose white Greta Garbo hat. Not so long ago, I had imagined myself wearing it to work at the School. Two little feet under the huge white hat, stomping along on the sand—I would never grow up into it. Roberta already had.

I want to stretch through the sleeping part of my face to

against the wind, a kite's not free or beautiful—it's only taut string.

Now it is night; the Trip will begin soon. I want to go dump my fears on Mary but she is working a few hours of the night shift at the Nursery. So I sit in my room, dreaming I am dead, then up and over to Ginny and Bebe's bedroom, listening to the girls discuss Ginny's tremendous bust.

"Was it hard doin' the strip, Gin?" Bebe is asking.

"Naw! It's great but you had to do a lot of exercises to keep your tits up."

"Could you swing the tassels?" Roberta wants to know. I go into the bathroom. When I come out, Ginny is standing in the middle of the room with her pajamas on, explaining she never got the knack of swinging the tassels in opposite directions.

Back into my room and close the door. Well, it's better than dying. I look in the mirror: "Keep your tits up," I think.

# 2.

# the trip: facing the fire

*Short Poem Written in Installments*

*Out of the loneliness and fear of this time*
*We can crave peace.*

*Out of the loneliness of this time*
*We can carve peace.*

*Out of this time*
*We can contain peace.*

# Indoctrination into trip

I scramble up the long steps into the Club. As usual, people are lounging around. The man at the Wedge is checking out cars, while others sit on two long sofas waiting quietly for the jitney. But tonight there's a shiver in the air. This is it, baby. Suddenly, it seems that my skirt is too short. Burlap robes are piled on a long table near the jitney waiting area, and a woman measures one for me.

"Do you have any valuables?" she says. We both laugh.

I'm Santa Claus, carrying my bag full of tooth brush and paste, flip flops, deodorant, soap, bathing suit, and a swim cap with a hole in it. The trick is to juggle all this, a pillow, and my Trip robe, and follow Mary downstairs to the locker room.

There's the familiar metallic sound of lockers clanging and the queer echoes. It's like being back in the YWCA and ten years old: I see the big girls with bras and I giggle with my girl friend.

We find two lockers. Cots have been set up, in case we want to sleep during the rest periods. "But I'm making a secret covenant, Mary, which I will share with you; not to close my ivory-colored lids *once* during the whole flight!" She laughs at me. "Oh, Barb, you're so melodramatic." It's true, I must do it. Saba told me I would learn more by going the whole forty-eight hours without sleeping. Besides, this is my last chance to learn something about Synanon.

Joan, Maureen, and Dorothy are fixing up their cots. I don't like to look at Dorothy. She's a lump of clay with two broken toothpicks stuck in. Impossible to talk to them with my stomach jumping this way, but one can sit down and watch. Pretty and scared; chattering—like women do when they're scared—endlessly, a great ocean roll of talk. Then Ruth calls to tell us it's time and to bring our pillows.

"What's a Shepherd?" I ask as we walk back to the main floor.

"Well, Barbara," Ruth explains, "it's someone who takes

care of you outside your Game times. The Trip has three different groups of people working on it—the Guides who lead the Games, the Trip Leader (Ted Dibble), who takes care of the general sessions, and the four Shepherds (two men, another woman, and myself) who take care of you during the free periods. By the way, who's your leader in your Games?"

"Mike Kaiser, I guess."

"You're lucky, Barb, he's a great guy! If you need anything in the locker room, just ask Sue or me."

"Oh," I say. Adding "how nice" would be fake and I'm not going to be fake during the Trip. But why did I eat that taco before coming here?

The Trip room is a lovely long place with a bar on one side where the Shepherds are standing. About sixty people are already seated on long sofas and on the rugs. Behind them are sliding doors leading out to a veranda that overlooks the sea.

I'm on the sofa near Midge, one of the women in my Mamas' and Papas' tribe. The men are still sitting on their pillows on the rug before us.

The neck of the fellow in front of me is a brown freeway of lines. What does each line mean, where do they all lead—how many times have they moved the neck in laughter, in tenseness, or tears? Unconsciously, I touch the back of my neck: it is very smooth.

Ted Dibble walks majestically into the room. He's wearing purple and gold robes. Each of the Game Guides is introduced and then seated on "thrones" in various parts of the room. Mike's robe is red, making his beard even darker. He must be about twenty-five and still all legs and arms; probably not even as smart as I. Ted is enjoying himself as he introduces the four Shepherds. Then he stills the laughter and goes to the portable blackboard.

"Now that the introductions are done, I'd like to welcome you to your Trip. The theme of this Trip is *Fiducia*." He writes it on the board awkwardly. "It means trust. You've got to allow yourself to be led during this Trip. Trust each of us and you will come to trust yourself. Even if you think that what you're asked to do is crazy, just act *as if*—then the trust will come. Act *as if* you trust and you'll get a lot out of this Trip."

Why do they always repeat everything twice? Do they really think we are all dingbats?

Ted begins to draw on the board. "This is each one of us.

Over a period of years, we build up hostilities toward ourselves and others. Perhaps these hostilities are based on a real hurt or failure in the past. On this hurt we build a huge network of pain; then, to protect ourselves, we add a nice wedge of hardness, emotional cement, to hold all this hostility and hurt in. "We end up looking something like this:

"If we can get a little emotionally free, a bit dissipated, we can take off our hard crust, and eventually clean out our hostility. It's then possible to come to terms with that original pain or fear or whatever it is."

He looks around the room carefully, then sits on his throne at the front. "You're going to go through a great deal in the forty-eight hours. And for most of you, because you will try a little *Fiducia,* it will be one of the most exciting experiences in your life. An experience that will be a departure point for you, because you'll clear out all that crap from your guts and begin to feel good. Feeling good is being free . . . And being free, folks, is being responsible." The room had narrowed down to 140 silent eyes on Ted.

"You gotta say to yourself, 'What's my fix? What keeps me from being free?' Emerson calls it 'the foolish face of praise,' meaning that ninety percent of consciousness is used for appearance sake only."

"On this trip you're going to *see* and *feel* what you've been missing. So live these few hours to the hilt! The Guides, the

Shepherds, all of us here, are going to ask a lot of trust from you. It's up to you to deliver, or miss the Trip . . . You'll have your Games and cerebrations, both of which will feed you pieces of information. You'll have free time, too, but I advise you to sleep as little as you possibly can. Don't sell your power short: you need a lot less sleep than you think. Later on, I'll give you some hints on that . . . The sauna, the pool, any part of the Club you'd like to use is yours . . . But one warning: speak to no one except fellow members of your Trip." He lights a cigarette and smiles.

"Now—how many people are married or engaged in this room?" About a third of the people raise their hands. "I'm going to ask you to exercise your *Fiducia.* From now on, all people who have a relationship with one another are on a ban. That's Synanon's language, meaning that you treat each other as strangers from now on." No one questions this, and Ted goes on. "You're perhaps going to know many moments that will give you an insight about feeling good and being free—" He looks at us carefully. "Then Dennis Resino, over here, one of the Game Guides, is going to give each of you a manila envelope. In it will be a notebook and pen. Write down what you learn so that when the feeling of the Trip wears off, you'll still find information on how to live . . . As Dennis calls out each of your names, I'll give you the envelope, and you'll come up to the front of the room to get it."

Dennis self-importantly lifts up the first envelope, calls out "Gregory," and hands it to Ted. A small, gray-haired man walks up to the front of the room.

"All right, Gregory," Ted smiles and hands him the envelope, "I want you to make the sound of your favorite animal and we'll try to guess who it is."

"A—any animal?" Gregory can barely swallow. We look at one another. People are moving around; the flip-flop of their sandals can be heard against the floor. My own fears and resentment somehow fix on Mike Kaiser's last words in our pre-Trip game: "Now don't worry folks, it'll be lots of fun! Especially for the women, watching the men trying to keep their genitals from falling out."

"I'm sorry—I—I just can't think of any," the man said. Ted

blinks a couple of times. "Well, try a dog." The man seems to cower against the blackboard.

"I can't do it. I just can't say it." He looks beseechingly at Ted. Poor trembling old man, can't even say bow-wow. Finally, Ted tells him to sit down; the little game goes on. I pretend I'm a snake; they easily guess it . . . I sit down, feeling sorry for whoever's in the group with Gregory.

Suddenly, it's awfully hot and I'm feeling rather dizzy. At last, it's a coffee break; we go outside and I get some tea. The small white cup seems unbearably heavy in my hands. I sit down in a deck chair on the veranda. Someone comes over.

"Hi, Sister. Good talk."

"Hi. Yeah." My lips are the size of my pillow. I try to get up. Everything is smearing before me—coffee, tea, smoke, *fiducia*. Good God, to faint in front of all these people!

"Get her to a bathroom!" Oh no, I'll miss my Trip, have to go home . . . I can't find the door. "Excuse me." A woman's brushing her hair. Oh God, this is so ghastly. Once in the Novitiate at Christmas, we were so hungry I ate tacos and tamales, little sweet pickles, and chocolate candy, and then I vomited. Horrible. I hadn't ever heard of a novice being a glutton.

But honest, all I've eaten tonight is one nineteen-cent taco and now it's going down the toilet. A kind, Mexican woman is with me; she takes me back to the Trip room. Everyone is wandering around. No one seems to notice as I sink quietly in a soft chair. People are starting to sit down again. Ted plays a bomb tape and the people quiet down.

"What're we gonna do now?" a guy asks.

"Goin' to have a cerebration," someone answers.

"A what?"

"It's a word that means we're goin' to listen to some tapes and talk about them."

There's a cool breeze on my neck. Things are clearing up a bit, but I'm still rather shaken up.

Ted adjusts his purple robes. "All right, folks, we're going to listen to the first Trip tape given by Chuck Diedrich . . . Take notes; he'll say a lot of things you'll like to remember."

So this was Chuck himself, the founder, oracle, boss, president of the firm, the old man. His voice is a gruff growl at life, but I listen with every pore open and get almost his whole talk verbatim.

"When a person's tired, dissipated—the ego will go into some changes. A Trip can lead you to many more valuable experiences than you ever believed. It is primarily an education experience—to find yourself, your fellowmen, and the nature of reality. So let things happen to you; let learning and data come into you.

"Three main points to remember during your Trip:

"1. You will have an eight-hour cycle on this Trip, not the usual twenty-four-hour one. It will be like the day on a sailing vehicle—four hours on, four hours off; or, in other words, four hours of activity and four hours of free time. Thus, in forty-eight hours, you will actually live six days.

"2. At the end of this rainbow, there will be a pot of gold. You come in here with a sense of annihilation and encapsulation from your fellowman. Through dissipation, or long hours of activity without very much sleep, we hope to bring about in you a conscious state of inebriation. We want to get you loaded without acid . . . If you're open to the Trip, you'll get a feeling of extreme closeness—you'll be very forgiving, very eager to get inside someone else, and let him get inside you.

"3. The Trip can become a reference point of life for you—because for six days you were able to share the miracle of consciousness, the miracle of life, with one another.

"No longer will you lead what Thoreau called a life of 'quiet desperation.' Suddenly, despite all our hangups, we no longer try to escape from life—but to get into it more!

"The few hot minutes of consciousness that you'll have—don't waste them! All man's endeavors are a search for himself . . . We are all searching for a life that is moving toward the *center of things*—your center of things.

"What we want to do in this Trip is to make life real. It can't be figured out in your head; books won't do it—all searching leads to the same question: *to be or not to be.*

"By my hangups, I've killed myself. I killed the human part of me. Now, I'm engaged in the search—and folks, the search itself is the fun, the goal is meaningless.

"I must enjoy the Trip, day by day. Remember—I have

more ahead of me than I do behind me . . . I face each new day standing on top of the isle of my experience; thus, each new day becomes a bigger day.

"We live in a world that can exist as long as we are interested in its existence.

"We are rigid, patterned, time-bound people in this world . . . WE JUST HAVE TO LOOSEN UP. Let your ego go—you might learn something!

"I was a real hostile son-of-a-bitch until I found a place for my hostility. Now I hate prejudice but not the quality of prejudice, I hate cruelty but not cruel people, I hate greed but not greedy people. During this Trip, you, too, might learn a place for your own hostility.

"These are the possibilities that you might come across during this Trip:

a few changes in your value system
a few notions about life
a few new viewpoints about people

—and also, great targets for your hostility. For it seems to me, you can't have much love unless you have an equal amount of hate.

"You know, our species is a really dumb species—we kill and eat and suck life out of each other. And I don't need smart pills or smart juice to help me work on this discovery . . . I'm finding out as fast as I can how Goddamn dumb I am.

"If you do your best, you can't fail . . . And remember, every time you find an answer, you get another question. If you didn't, you'd die of boredom in ten minutes. You wouldn't want anything—total satiation, total sobriety—it would be Hell. You wouldn't even want the next breath.

"So, as the old A.A. slogan puts it, 'It doesn't take much of a man to make this program, it takes all of him.' "

Ted raises his hand. "There's a lot of meat in that tape. But now we're going to hear a tape by Sidney Poitier reading Plato's 'Our World, a Cave'—listen carefully because we're going to have a discussion on it."

"Human beings live in an underground cave. Their backs are to the light. They cannot see the fire in the center of the cave. They can see only the shadows. Thus, truth comes to be a shadow; of true images, they know nothing.

"But one man wants freedom. He looks toward the light and he experiences sharp pain. Once upon a dark cave, he thought the shadows reality, the sun unreal. But now he knows . . . He will no longer fit in; their honors will not be his.

"When he comes back out of the sun, he will no longer see as they see. His eyes will be dark. They will say,

" 'He went up and down, he came back without his eyes. It is better not even to think of ascending.' "

Listening, my mind seems suddenly to split in two. I'm on two mental tracks: Barbara, the Trip member, and Barbara, somewhere else listening to the story of the shadow people. At first, I don't understand; the story is too simple. I merely think: "O.K., great men have eyes darkened by their vision. Men look into them and search for a meaning. They come away seeing nothing, saying 'this man has the dark eyes of a dog.' " The fact is that I can't see past my own shadows, the tilt of my mind, my precious images. But what about the cave I'm living in; what if my God-talk obscures God, what if my building of steeples obliterates life? Wouldn't I rather make ritual with my back to the fire than face it quietly and completely? Perhaps I am the shadow, and these people will be the fire. But what will happen if I come out of the cave?

# The hand touch

Sitting in the lonely cave of myself, I hear bits and pieces of the discussion. Ted is saying that we measure ourselves by what we are or want, not by our possibilities—that which is beyond our own shadow: "This Trip is your chance to go beyond your own shadow. *Give it all you can.*" He takes a few drags from his cigarette.

"You'll have a little free time now. If you begin to find yourself getting tired, try this method: Take a cold shower, as cold as you can stand, then take a hot shower, really hot, then take another cold shower, and go immediately to the Sauna. It's what we call expansion and contraction. You'll be refreshed, if you take it correctly. But it's essential that you take a cold, hot, cold shower before the Sauna . . . All right, folks, the Shepherds will now lead you down to the lockers."

We file out. This expansion-contraction idea seems exciting; wonder if it works? They're not taking us to the lockers, though, but to the couch area of the main floor. Someone's arranged the couches so that they face each other. We pile onto them and kibbitz. So great not to be a nun symbol—no big discussions about Cardinal McIntyre, birth control, the Church; just young girl Barbara in a group picture with others. We play charades; I get my chance to show off. Then Ruth tells us to go out on the main dance floor.

The Club is extraordinarily quiet. Having used the night only for sleep, I'm not used to being awake now. The night is all hollow; voices echo around me, everything seems strangely lonely. It must be very late. Ruth puts on the Sounds of Synanon Band's Hoopla Album.

Once, before I entered the convent, my brother took me to a bar. We actually won a dance contest, which entitled us to a pitcher of beer per night for a week. Never got to enjoy the beer; that was the week I went to St. Joseph's Novitiate, and since then there's been little dancing. How I miss it! But I couldn't seem to do it well at Synanon; I was a tin nun with nails in my joints.

Tonight, however, as the Hoopla starts, it is like being a great athlete as his whole body bends into the throwing of a ball. I am so completely attached to the music that wherever it goes in the room, I can go too. And I go, I go . . .

The dance over, Ruth tells us to sit in a large circle on the floor, and face the person we are sitting next to. I'm sitting next to New Yorker Sean, who seems almost as much a big mouth as Mike Kaiser.

"Now," Ruth continues. "I want you to close your eyes and compose yourselves. Move a little bit closer to each other so that your knees are touching." Frankly, I'm scared. "Better. Now concentrate on the pressure of another's knee upon yours—cut yourself off from everything else." Sean's knees feel bony, good . . .

"Take the person's hand into yours." I can't find Sean's hands! He finds mine, quiets them. "I want you," Ruth continues, "to discover all that you can about that person from their hands. Speak to each other; listen with your whole self."

*Hands that wash and cannot wash away the warmth and sweat of sin. Hands that roll into tight balls with laughter or hatred. Ragged hands that beg. Thick hands that become worn and shaky. Rotted hands. Beginning hands—like Sean, like me.*

We are awkward yet nimble with one another, spreading our fingers like paired butterflies.

My fingers walk up and down the ruts and jungles on Sean's hands; yes, in this one person there is enough mystery to last me forever. I say to him, come play with me; I say, no; that I love you; I say I'm afraid of fireflies, that the sea is the land's echo; I ask, who is God? And to all my questions, Sean answers. He tells me, yes; he says people can really ice skate on deserts; that the moon is the universe's monocle; that I shouldn't be afraid of the Cyclops; that fireflies are made to be used as night lights; that he loves me; that God must have hands—how else could he touch us?

When we open our eyes, Sean and I have nothing to do but smile and say the dance is over, thank-you words. But the words brush against our faces like bats. And we feel foolish, so we turn to watch the others.

Liz's withered legs are painfully wrapped Indian-fashion;

her frightened fluttering hands are searching a man's hands. Yet she has found peace in this hollow space in the night.

What hands go through—the dirty daily jobs, the addict popping his high, the thief stealing his goods, the prostitute arousing her game. Yet they will always be more expressive than words, because they speak in feelings. Hands don't crush us with ideas. They would never tell big Matt over there, "You're black and probably smell, and how in the hell do you ever comb your hair?" They simply say, "Hi, I'd like to get to know you. You don't need to account for this huge scar running down the side of your hand; it's you, so I love the scar."

My hands are still heavy with Sean. I move back to the side and look at them. If we could just do that with every part of our body. Hello elbow, you're not ugly. Hi there, kneecap, how's the roughness going? don't be ashamed. That you, earlobe? But perhaps it doesn't matter.

When I am old, almost finished with the dirty work dragging me down, let Sean still be a wound in my hands. When they are rotted and shake, as if I'm always keeping time to an inner music, let him be a part of my wrinkles and longing. Let me go through life with Sean heavy on my hands.

# *The first eight-hour game*

## I. Gregory

You've seen people like Gregory on park benches. He's the one shaking like a leaf beneath his newspaper wall. He doesn't feed the pigeons—they might bite. He may try to lose his sadness in wine, but he hasn't learned the trick—it won't fit down the narrow neck of the bottle. When he smashes the bottle on his head, it won't break. He's always the one standing, sitting, walking alone wherever I happen to be.

It's easy to make up comic stories about him, trying to imagine what experiences drove him to what he is today. But I remember visiting a distant relative who lived on the side of a great highway. His proud possession is not his wife or land, cats or the lace patches on his furniture; it is one small notebook dirtied by the touch of his shaking hands. He holds it high in the afternoon sun as it slants through his front room window.

"What are all those slashes and lines?" I ask him quietly.

He answers with a gesture of bone and sinew that takes in the window and the highway beyond. "The cars," He smiles proudly.

"The what?"

"I count the cars." At the time, he had already marked down 170,000 cars in some private contest with himself.

Hearing Gregory make the sound of a castrated dog, I wonder if he's spent twenty-five years marking down lines and slashes since he was a freshman in college. But I cannot really feel pity; I only ask: Why did they take out Vance from our game and replace him with this horrible little caricature of a man?

For Gregory life "is but a sleep and a forgetting" of that terrible day in the amphitheater. How his steps echo in the hall! He runs a little, it is the scurry of a tiny rat who hides in the nearest empty seat. Why had he gone away to school? But above all, why had he consented to take a speech class? He ducks his head and turns up his collar.

The speech teacher is miles below him, standing before a huge fish bowl. His elephantine hand fumbles in the bowl and brings out horrendous challenges for each poor freshman. Did he call his name? His soles are peanut butter. Each step sticks to the bread floor. The teacher's giant hand makes a shadow on Gregory's tiny body. Gregory is sure his pants are cut off: everyone can see his shaking knees. The teacher reaches in the bowl. What he pulls out is juicy mucus, bird dung, dog dew, and coagulated blood. And Gregory has to hold it in his hand as his mind vomits and he can't say anything for three minutes.

"And that's why you can't go bow-wow?" Mike sneers.

"It was horrible. Three solid minutes of silence. A hundred faces looking at me holding this grotesque thing!"

"Can a speech teacher get away with that?" I ask.

Mike looks at me like I'm a fool. He turns back to Gregory. "Gregory, what did you pull out of the fish bowl?"

One small folded piece of paper with blue print expressing a job he couldn't make himself do.

"So for twenty-five years you've been unable to speak in front of people?" I ask.

"Of course, I can speak. But not when I'm asked to make a fool out of myself—so that everyone will laugh at me."

"We're not laughing because we don't like you, Gregory," John says.

"You're so afraid," Dorothy adds.

"Yes, I am. I wish I had your courage."

"Well, show a little," Mike prods. "Get up and go bow-wow."

Gregory shivers a little. "I can't."

Mike's face hardens. "Get up and go bow-wow."

*"I can't."*

*"Stand up, Gregory."* He stands up. *"Now open your fuckin' mouth and say bow."*

"Bo." A squeak.

"Force that Bo deeper into your throat."

"I can't."

"All right, Gregory," Mike sighs. "Say Awful."

"Awful."

"Now say Awf."

"Awf."

"Now go Arf. Arf."

"Arf. Arf." We applaud.

"All right, Gregory. Sit down. Fine. That's enough, I'm not here to play psychiatrist . . ." Mike lights a cigarette.

"But I *am* a psychiatrist," Gregory murmurs with a slight smile.

Mike almost drops the cigarette. "A what?" Sean whoops.

"Not exactly, of course, but I counsel students at a university."

I think I'm going to get sick again.

## II. Kent E. Long and Irma

Synanon is a subway. It barrels down the long tunnel of life; either you make it, with the crowd pushing, cajoling, or you miss it. Either way, it's painful. If you miss it, you might get caught in the jaws of its closing door, or lose a purse, or even an arm or leg. If you make it, it might turn out to be the wrong train. Then you end up in an alien land and are lost.

I look hard at Kent. I'm wondering if he's making or missing the subway. He had been with us on the pre-Trip. Only Gregory and black Matt are new to us. Kent reminds me of some medieval knight with his careful moustache and goatee, his great body and his slumbering eyes. They attack him because his father is rich and Kent had conveniently taken over the family car business. He recently married.

"Have you ever two-timed Susie?" Mike lifts one eyebrow.

"Yeah. Before we started playing Games at Synanon."

"Why? Wasn't she enough for you, asshole?"

"Yeh—but whenever I failed . . ."

"Kent E. Long, Jr., failing?" Sean's voice is goading, not questioning.

"Yeh, motherfucker, I fail!" Kent's face is red.

"Get to the point," Mike inserts.

"Well, when things got me down—I'd go out and see how easy I could get a lay."

"Was it?" Sean asks.

"Sure, easy."

There is a long pause, his hair is damp and the points of his chin (it was a motion in our pre-Trip game that he cut his goatee off) are all pink and rough. He keeps shifting in his chair, fixing his robe, clearing his throat.

We can't seem to get through to him. Mike has tried everything. He's made fun of him, yelled at him, called him proud ass—but Kent is untouched. Why'd he come along on this Trip? Maybe it will help him sell cars better.

There was this ten-minute chapter of a movie serial I saw when I was about the size of my popcorn bag. The theater crackled with excitement as we watched the hero and heroine stand by the snapping crocodile. Are we Kent's crocodiles? Anyway, looking at him eat a doughnut, I have the sense that something is going to happen.

Mike has gone out of the room for a minute; it must be moving toward day. Outside, birds are bothering barking dogs and the cotton candy and popcorn machines are warming up. I wish I could walk down the promenade and buy some buttered corn-on-a-stick. We've been in here so long, I can hardly follow much of what is said. What more can happen to us here? The feeling returns of a hero and heroine slowly descending into the crocodile waters . . .

The mind filters. Now it's Irma, the Jewish lady, who has a long thin neck with a bob of a head on top and eyes that are popping out. She has two daughters, and has recently separated from her husband.

Mike begins the inquisition:

"Did he want to move out?"

"Yes."

"Bullshit. Didn't you tell him to get out?" Mike lights a new cigarette.

"I told him we should be apart for awhile—that our life together was becoming too much."

"Did he want to move out?"

"I don't know how he felt."
"Bullshit."
"—even if he didn't want to, he went anyway."
"Why?"
"Because—you have a saying for it here . . ."
"Well—what is it?" Mike leans forward.
"He has no balls."
Laughter. "Maybe you have them all," Mike answers.

After that, I stop listening. Typical Jewish mother; dismiss her as selfish, domineering, sinister—comic. Sitting alongside Kent, I'm falling asleep when his arm stiffens. It's Ted Dibble with a young woman.

"Susie," Kent says. It's his wife.

She is given a chair in the circle and promptly begins to cry.

"Well, Susie . . ." Ted gets seated again, pulls his robe down.

Kent is sweating horribly. I'd like to get out, go to the bathroom, buy popcorn. Susie blows her nose.

"I just had to say it, Kent."

Kent swallows. "What—what, Susie?"

"I'M JUST SICK OF THE WHOLE DAMN THING!" She is crying again. "I—I don't trust you, I'm never sure about what you'll do . . . You used to make it with a lot of girls . . . You told me you've stopped . . . HAVE YOU?"

"I—I told you I had. I stopped when we started playing the Games." His face is very red.

"Why don't you tell the truth, Kent, for once in your goddamn life, why don't you tell the truth!" she yells.

"I *am* telling you the truth."

"You're not, you're not!" She blows her nose. "I had to tell it, Kent—I couldn't stand it any longer . . ."

"What—whatdyamean?"

"The marijuana." We look at Kent—maybe he's going to faint.

"I—I," he stammers.

Susie seems to gather courage. "How every goddamn night for the last three months you've been getting out of the goddamn bed and rolling a goddam joint."

Kent's hair is matted on his head; he looks like a big red balloon. I'd touch him, but I can't stop crying; Susie crumples into her chair.

"Well, Kent E. Long, what do you have to say to us?" Ted's voice is particularly quiet.

"I—I couldn't sleep."

"Many people can't."

"I felt tense. It wasn't a habit."

"Yes, that's what you said, Kent. You told me not to tell it in Games and we kept on lying, and I'm sick of it—sick of the whole goddamn lie!" Susie yells.

"So you make a contract with your wife—three months of games, three months of marijuana and lies. Bet you feel real good right now," Mike says.

"I—I feel horrible."

"You should, Kent, you know Synanon's rules." Ted spits it out.

"Yes."

"Asshole! What are they?" Mike yells.

"No acid, grass, or heroin at any time, no alcohol before a Game if you're a square . . ." Kent says them thickly; they must weigh down his mouth.

"So in all fairness we should kick you out of this Trip and Synanon."

"Yes," Kent agrees, staring straight ahead.

"Don't be so goddamn noncommittal, Kent E. Long! You've had everything you've ever wanted, motherfucker, and now it's the end. *You got caught, Kent!* We all see you for what you are —fuckin' other women when you've only been married six months, smoking grass, lying to everyone at Synanon. Do you know what I'd like to do?" Ted yells.

"What?" Kent blinks a few times.

"I'd like to go downstairs and call the cops. I'd like to have them take a peek in your honeymoon cottage and find the tin can of grass and give Mr. Kent E. Long Senior's son five years in prison. And do you know why I'd like to do it?"

"Why?" He can barely get the words out.

"Because you're the goddamn motherfucker type who gets away with it!"

"I—I haven't gotten away with it."

"No, baby, you haven't," Ted considers a moment. "Well, since we don't have any fuzz present we're going to avail ourselves of a little American custom—"

"Lynching?" Sean suggests.

"Shut up, teenager!" Ted yells. Sean ducks. "We're going to try you. Mike and I will be the judge. Matt—Fran, John, Sean—Barbara, all the Synanon residents in this room will be the jury . . . We will vote whether you will leave right now or be allowed to remain until the end of the Trip."

*"Please—please let us stay!"* Susie cries hysterically.

The hero and the heroine descend into the crocodile waters. I listen to Kent's defense and Ted's rebuttal. Susie makes no excuses. We vote.

"I—I'm sorry, sorry," Kent is blubbering. "Thank you for letting me stay the Trip—I need it—need Synanon." He buries his red face in his hands.

"All right, Kent—at the end of the Trip we'll tell you if you'll be accepted back into Synanon. Right now you're no longer a member . . . All you got is the Trip." Ted and Susie leave the room.

## III. Matt

A sense of sleeplessness comes, and the feeling that one was born on a freeway with nothing to do at night but listen to the honks and blowouts of people's lives. Listen to baby-faced, black Matt:

"*The past is past*—don't want to talk about it."

"Well then, why are you on the Trip, Matt?" Mike leans back, waiting.

"I dunno, man . . . I had to do something . . . I asked to go into a Stew but they wouldn't let me—told me to come here."

"What's the problem?"

"I dunno—feel like I've made no progress at Synanon."

"What about Jan?"

"What about her?"

"I hear you have a problem about deciding to get married or not."

"Don't love her."

"How long have you had a relationship with her?"

"Eighteen months."

"Long time, Matt."

"Well, how long have you been going with Diane?"

"About as long."

"Long time, Mike." We laugh. Matt leans forward. "Why don't you marry Diane?"

"I wouldn't even begin to think about that until she and I had gone through a Stew together and really faced each other and found out where we both are," Mike answered.

"I wanta ask you something, Mike."

"What, Matt?"

"Once we were friends—once—well, you're the one that got my choral group its first jobs."

"Yeah—so? You have a good group."

"You mean that?"

"Yeh—sure."

*"Then why the hell did you blackball us from the San Francisco Fair?"* Matt is screaming.

"Well, Matt—we had so many acts—I didn't blackball you. Frankly, there wasn't room." Mike is calm.

"*Bullshit!* We worked for months on the stuff. You knew we were coming, why didn't you tell us earlier?"

"Well, Matt. The Fair's so big now, we didn't think of it."

"*Bullshit!* You knew about us—you just wanted to hurt twelve people who worked their asses off!"

"All right, Matt. Baby, you just weren't good enough, if you want it between the eyes! We wanted to give you more time . . . And why don't you tell the folks how you told your people . . ."

"Whatdyamean?"

"*Asshole—tell them how you did it!*"

Matt begins to look sheepish. "Well—I, I just told them we weren't needed at the Fair."

"Fuck you! You know that's a lie. Let me tell them how you did it, since you don't have the guts." Mike stands and holds an imaginary letter in his hands. "Well, folks . . . those Synanon-director racist assholes up in S.F. have done it to us again . . . they've stuck a knife through our backs . . . don't trust them anymore."

"I didn't say that!"

"Well, Matt you must have—because two of your fabulous choral group split Synanon after that gas . . ."

"I dunno, Mike—I dunno what to do."

"Think hard, Matt, you've still got time . . ."

## IV. Fran and Picture

Enter Fran, the ex-whore.

"What does your father do, Fran?"

"He's a saleman; he was a marine." She nervously fiddles with her reddish-brown hair.

"Tough?"

"Yeah—very. He didn't *want* me to get away with anything." She crosses her long legs.

"But you did."

"Yeah."

"Your mother?"

"Weak—kinda like Joan. But I loved her."

Joan is sniffling again. John Barry leans forward, "Do you like men, Fran?"

"Of course."

"One would think you got very tired of them with your job." John smiles.

"I like them just fine."

"Do you think that you know everything there is to know about them?"

"How do you mean?"

"Physically, my dear."

Fran laughs. "Yes, asshole! Of course!"

John looks around the room. "Go up to that blackboard and draw a picture of a man."

Mike looks at him curiously but lets him continue.

Fran doesn't want to go. Shyly, she smiles, "Well—why?"

"Do it, my dear."

She gets up. At Synanon you don't procrastinate very long. She draws a stick figure man.

"Hey, Fran! That's no man!" Mike understands John's scheme.

"Why, yes it is," Fran says.

"A head, trunk, two arms, and a pair of legs doesn't make a man, Fran," Irma laughs harshly.

"Draw the genitals, Fran," John says gently.

"A—what?" Fran gasps. "I can't . . ."

"We just want to observe how much you know about a man."

"Oh, all right." So she draws the penis and the testes, right there, right on the board. If my Superior could only see me now, sinking in my seat, trying to find a collar on my robe to turn up! But I can't take my eyes away from the blackboard because there's something wrong with her drawing. And I start laughing to myself, remembering how I know it's not to scale.

John carefully appraises the board.

"What's your verdict, Dr. John?" Mike smirks.

"You're finished now, Fran? You're quite sure you're correct?" John says.

"Yes, of course."

I can't stand it any longer. "Wait," I blurt out. "It's wrong! Even *I* know it's wrong!"

"Well, go up and change it!" Mike laughs, too.

I'm shaking all over. Hell no, I won't go! Hell, yes, I best! Remembering Gregory and the bow-wow, I don't dare procrastinate. Up to the blackboard, certain that half of my robe is ripping off, fixing my bangs. Fran hands me the chalk. And I draw *it* and two little testes, but I make sure to draw one smaller than the other.

John smiles at Fran. "That is correct, Barbara. You see, Fran, one testis is always smaller than the other."

"Oh," and now Fran is laughing.

"Need I say more?" John's case rests.

Burning all over, I can barely find my chair; everyone's talking and laughing around me. They'd laugh more if they realized how I knew. I was sitting in a car two days before I came to Synanon, waiting for Sister Maura. On the seat was a book entitled *Facts of Life for Children.* I'll just have to read a more advanced book when I go home.

# Interlude on the beach

The Shepherds lead us out into the day. We're told to take off our flipflops and follow the leader out to the ocean. How the people stare—fifty brown robes freckling the white sand. The cold salt water sets me on edge; suddenly I can do anything, anything. I spread the she-points of my body. See Sean, see Fran, I am a windmill, a sailplane, a carousel!

"All right, Trip people," Ruth claps her hands. "Make a large circle just outside Synanon's beach-front fence." When we sit, I notice that I am next to Midge again. I ask her how her Trip's going.

She answers, "Marvelous! Not even tired, old woman of forty that I am!"

Ruth leads a woman into the center. "Close your eyes," she tells her. She starts molding her body as if it were clay. She pulls her arms out straight, and gently begins to shape them until they seem to be holding a burden. Then gradually, she lowers the woman until she is kneeling on the sand, offering flowers to a god. Slowly, other couples join her. One person closes his eyes and is clay, the other is artist.

Midge is watching a man shape a woman into a child and his butterfly.

"See the child flying his butterfly?"

"What?" Midge looks at me.

"I mean kite—see the kite?" I point to the sculpture.

Are we in a zoo? Beach people are sitting, standing, surrounding us to stare. The children nibble popcorn and throw sand on us. "What *are* they doing?" "Crazy dope addicts." "Drunk—at noon!" "There oughta be a law!"

Sean is turning Sister Mary into Artemis. He gently makes her bend her legs, then carefully shapes her arms to hold the bow, then he moves her hands back and forth until she finally does it by rote, as if she were a hand in a precision timepiece.

There is a beautiful dark-haired woman coming out of her cocoon. A Negro does a love-dance around her, always shaping her, for she is his clay. Finally, she holds her white arms to the sea with his black hallelujah.

Ruth asks for more volunteers and Midge and I go into the center. I close my eyes and the sun and noise coalesce into a great warm wheel spinning around me. I feel Midge's hands shaping me, and the pain of my body.

Her hands tell me to hold my position but move slowly. I move on my knees and open my eyes slightly: only sand and the feet and legs of people. We must be a line of living statues, surrounded by the sea and Synanon.

A hand beckons me. I follow blindly. I kneel and am told to stretch out my arms. Other hands are placed on mine—I'm not afraid. The hands pull me toward the center of an invisible circle, then lift, lift toward the sky. I open my eyes. The hands pointing to the sky are of different colors. We have become a spiral.

We laugh and my hair gets in my eyes. Good, *good.* We sit again in our circle; I am made of clear water.

Ruth begins a story. "Once upon a time, there was a little boy who lived by a great sea. Each afternoon, he'd run by the sea with his little dog, Clover. One day he found a bottle with a message inside it." She points to Sean.

" 'Well,' said the little boy, 'I can't read. So's I better take it to my Granddad who can read it to me.' " And Sean points to Gregory. The people in my Game go white. No scene, no goddamn bow-wow scene, here! Not after the warmth, the wheel!

Gregory twitches like a sandcrab. He clears his throat. "Sure—a—sure, my Grandson, I'll read it to you. It says, 'Whoever reads this note is entitled to a wonderful adventure. An adventure that will begin as soon as you lift the bottle to your eyes and look through . . .' " and then he points to someone else.

Gregory's face—it looked as if Synanon has handed him a bottle with a message in it. At first he is too frightened to follow. Then, he picks up the old bottle, squints his good eye, and looks through. What do you see old man, what do you see?

"All things in the sun are sun" (W. Stevens).

# Cerebration on Emerson

I blink rapidly as we come into the Club. Vance sits down next to me on the long sofa. Everyone is taking loudly and swirling around us, as a brunette girl leans toward me: "Are you really a nun?"

I decide to tease her: "Are you scared?"

"But I've never talked to a nun before . . ."

"Exciting, isn't it?" Vance laughs lightly. But she keeps on talking of habits and Sister Corita and all the meeting-a-modern-nun talk. I want Vance to leave, yet I want him to stay. One side of my hip is touching him, burning. Half of me is leaning toward him, while the other half is involved with the others in the lounge. I want to dance around and talk with everyone, and still be near Vance, silent. Black and white clown that I am, half a nun-thing, half Barbara. Celibate love. In the convent we call it non-exclusive love, an openness, an embracing of the world. Half of me is peaceful, reaching out, gayly, to everyone in the room. Half is magnetized (exclusively) upon Vance. He excuses himself. Sighing, I ask Ruth, where are we going now?

"Cerebrations. In your Game room." I walk upstairs with Joan and Fran. We sit down casually, wondering if we'll be able to talk, not fight.

"I thought it might be interesting to read through Emerson's essay on 'Self-Reliance' and then cerebrate," Mike says as he hands out mimeo sheets: sixteen pages, will I be able to stay awake?

Each of us reads a page; it is painful to listen to, like a line of people doing a dance together, some awkward, some graceful; all pulled down and held together by a common hesitancy.

> If any man consider the present aspects of what is called by distinction *society*, he will see the need of these ethics. The sinew and heart of man seem to be drawn out, and we are become timorous, desponding whimperers. We are afraid of truth, afraid of fortune, afraid of death, and afraid of each other.

> Our age yields no great and perfect persons. We want men and women who shall renovate life and our social state; but we see that most natures are insolvent, cannot satisfy their own wants, have an ambition out of all proportion to their practical force and do lean and beg day and night continually. Our housekeeping is mendicant, our arts, our occupation, our marriages, our religion, we have not chosen, but society has chosen for us. We are parlor soldiers. We shun the rugged battle of fate, where strength is born.

Mike lights a cigarette. "As you can tell, folks, the gist is a life of simple reinforcement or self-reliance. You've got to have what Emerson calls 'self-trust.' Do you see where on the last page, he says, 'Some favorable event raises your spirit, and you think good days are preparing for you. Do not believe it. Nothing can bring you peace but the triumph of principles.' In other words, you've got to 'do your work and you shall reinforce yourself.' "

I'm not convinced. "But, Mike, isn't just 'doing your work' what Emerson calls 'the hobgoblin of little minds,' loved by little people?"

He smiles. "Sure, if your work is always outside of yourself and not in your guts. That's why Synanon has Games, not to kill a person, but to force him to see the truth, to get inside and wiggle around a bit."

"But how can you *force* someone to see truth?" John inserts quietly. "After all, isn't truth relative?"

Maureen moves heavily in her chair. "I think that truth is reality as it's real to you."

Sean sits up. "Hey! I found what Emerson said about Games, listen . . . 'We come to them who weep foolishly, and sit down and cry for company, instead of imparting to them truth and health in rough electric shocks, putting them once more in communication with their reason.' Ol' Emerson's kinda up to date, huh, Mike?" He laughs.

"Yes he is, Sean. Let's see if anyone can find what he says about contract games—it's somewhere on page ten." Mike sits back. You'd think it was a race. Finally, John finds it: "Let us enter into the state of war, and wake Thor and Woden, courage and constancy, in our Saxon breasts. This is to be done in our smooth times by speaking truth. Check this lying hospitality and lying affection."

Mike continues, "In other words, folks, we've got to break our contract with each other, yes, but most of all—break it with ourselves. You come into a game, see, you make your ass real comfortable, a little game of Thor and Woden begins, electric verbal shocks everywhere, and then you split, right Matt?"

"Yeh, Mike—now you're talkin' so's I can understand."

"Yeh! But what happens when you split, leave the game? What's the purpose of a game anyway? What d' ya think, Fran?"

"To dump," she answers.

John raises his hand. "Or in other words, as Emerson puts it succinctly, to 'bring the past for judgment into the thousand-eyed present, and live ever in a new day.' " He rests.

"Man, I don't understand a word you say," Matt says.

Joan smiles, "Yes, John, why can't you speak simply."

John is angered, "My dear Joan, I was merely—"

"This ain't a game, folks! We've come to learn, so shut your yaps!" Mike yells. "A game is played to cut you off from fakery, from cocksucking the world, and tries to make you go it straight arrow." Mike goes to the blackboard, and writes, "Self-reliance —the game."

He goes on, "That's the whole point—self-reliance as an outgrowth of the game—but it's usually missed because in the Synanon Game, by and large, action is not taken."

Mike is beginning to make sense so I take notes: "Emerson speaks a great deal about the self-dependent, self-derived man," he continues. "This is a man who exercises, uses his free will. And by the way, what is free will?"

I raise my hand quickly, but he ignores me: "Free will is the realization that there are always alternatives, a man must make a choice. In fact, that's what action is . . ." He writes the word on the board. "Action involves closing the mind around one or more of these alternatives and consequently making a decision."

"Man, I'm learnin'," Sean exclaims, underlining the pages. "This is great, listen to this one: 'To be great is to be misunderstood'; or, how 'bout this one, 'Live no longer to the expectation of these deceived and deceiving people with whom we converse. Say to them, O father, O mother, O brother, O friend . . . "

Mike quickly moves to deflate: "O shut up, Sean, stop showing off!" "Let's get back to the point, folks . . . Emerson wants us to get away from silly conversations and to the point of life. But our problem, folks" (if he says "folks" one more time) "is words. For instance, nouns," he writes on the board, "are labels —take the word table. Adjectives, particularize a noun—for instance, brown table" (He's changed his approach; if he says "for instance" one more time—) ". . . verbs, are action. This is what we want in our life."

Yes, action, not barf. Mike's no smarter than I—I should be teaching this lesson myself. Yes, what I want in life is not Mike-mouth, but Vance. Soon the Saturday night show at the Club; soon, the Hoopla in our brown robes, and all I really want to do is sit by Vance. That's all. I want to wash my hands of all this. Who cares about truth anyway?

# Midnight hour

After watching the Saturday night show at the Club, we go upstairs for the "bewitching hour," the midnight festivities that Saba told me about so long ago. We crowd upstairs, Dot lagging behind as usual. I want to help, but remember her hatred of help. Mike Kaiser walks down the stairs toward us.

"Dorothy?" He puts his hands on her shoulders.

"Yes, Mike?" Nervously, she looks up at him.

"May I carry you, Dot?"

I stop short, afraid for them both, waiting for her answer: "Yes, Mike—please carry me."

At the top, the Shepherds tell us to form a long line outside the general Trip room and to remove our sandals.

I take off my flipflops obediently. The rug grits against my innocent feet. Can't even remember if I'm tired. One of the Shepherds blindfolds me, and the darkness wraps around my body. So this is to be the magic hour?

"Sit down like an Indian," someone whispers in my ear.

"Take the hands of the person on each side of you," the whisper waves in the darkness. I feel hands groping for my hands. Sean. I'm no longer afraid of hands because of him.

I can tell that one of the hands that touches mine has wiped many faces and tears, cleaned children, smacked bottoms, loved men—it must be Mo's. I squeeze it delightedly. The other hand—a man's? It is frightened, tries to cover up its nervousness by play—*I know who it is*—my hand must blush, it is James. Ugh, I want to walk away from him, hide my hand in the tufts of the carpet . . . Relax, Barbara, feel the perspiration come between us like the Red Sea.

Sitting between Maureen and James, hands tired, legs bent like Dot's, very little sound in the room. Shall I get bored? Perhaps I should pray—just focus on one small dot in the dark. Thank God, music, something to do. A woman is singing about Eleanor Rigby; how she lives in a rice dream, waiting for a wedding that remains just outside her window.

Something so long ago, I must have been very small. My older brother, probably about five, had been invited to a Christmas party—the memory remains dark, red, and embroidered with tinsel. I remember looking out the car window as we waited for my brother to come out. The house is up a slight incline; it is night and the house windows are warm. I want so much to go in, but haven't been invited. Is this what my life is? A peeping-Barbara, always standing outside lit houses?

All of them. The lonely people. Dust world. Sighing in the air, the people and trees creak. I am a scream with hands. Because we cannot speak nor bare the everyday silences, we cling to each other's bodies. It takes too long to come to know one another, so we delve into each other's secret places. "I want you" merely means your body; we usually make up our body before our mind.

So we reveal ourselves, spread our legs, move on. We go from cave to cave, until finally, we are bored, we know everything. Liars!—we haven't begun to understand. We haven't worked below the maze of touch and feel and me and you and ahh . . . The person, ourself, and others, is unexplored . . .

And I think of all the Father McKenzies who darn their socks while sitting on their velvet prie-deux. And give arching sermons to people whose ears are stuffed with holy cards. Oh God, I am back in my slot of a convent room, unable to sleep. I take my hand and brush my fingers against one leg; you'd think my hand and brush my fingers against one leg; you'd think my body is a guitar, the way one strum of a hand brings music. To hell with that game; I fold my hands neatly on the blanket while my throat's growing electric hairs. Me? I'm flying a kite with a key on its string, but can't take the shocks. So I watch my hand gambol in the shadows and make the finger, right in my bed. In the center of the convent, with all that baptismal water running through its pipes, and I'm longing for a man so bad my bed's like to split open and I'll fall through the night right onto the community car that's parked below me and shoot out to the moon, that vast, virginal hole in the sky.

There is that story told of Eleanor Rigby, that her life was snapped shut by a priest who read her like a boring book. And walked away, oh failed-savior, with dirty hands.

We are watching an improvised light show. I wipe my hands on my robe and lean back on a friendly man's legs. The screen looks as if various colored chemicals have been spilled all over glass, making fantastic shapes and sizes. A dream I once had—I was sure his body was a guitar, too. Back in the house, I smiled at my mother as he burned within me. Had she heard us through wide slats of the barn?

I sat down on the living room rug and began to play cards. He was leaning back on his elbows with his legs stretched out before him. The roughness of his jeans, the slant of sunlight on the Ace of Spades! I watch the light, trembling; does my mother know?

She sits on a low chair near us. "I have a bone to pick with you two," she begins.

He laughs, but I'm scared. She's heard us. Smelled us between the slats of other smells and other sounds. The way the wind whistled through us in that barn! Oh, life is full of holes. I cross my legs.

She asks quietly, "Which of you destroyed the rose bush outside?"

And sure enough, when we go to his room, we find a bunch of roses on his closet shelf.

Let it go on, let's see more dancing lights, let's hear more "Eleanor Rigby"; I want to be able to focus one inch to infinity —but they turn on the lights.

Ted is smiling at us. "I hope you liked the music and the light show that your Shepherds put on." I feel contained. Complete absorption. My body dances from ear to ear.

Ted continues, "Now we are going to impose a bit more on your trust. Mike Kaiser has invented a new game that we are going to watch being played. Mike? Carry on."

Mike hunches to the middle of the sixty or so people sitting on the floor. "Would the people in my Game please come out to the center of the room?"

We get up quickly and step out front. Mike holds up four different colored strings. "We're going to play a new game, a very serious game, called the String Game." I can't help laughing. He continues, "I hold four pieces of string, each of varying colors and lengths. For instance, this green string is four feet long—it's the shortest of the four—and it stands for *trust*. Fran, come here, hon . . ." She quickly obeys. "Now I let Fran hold one end of this string and she can give the other end to anyone in her game that she chooses." Fran motions for me to come, and I gladly take the end of the string.

Mike continues. "Now, Fran has three more strings to hold and she must give one end of each away. Here's an eight-foot, yellow string, which stands for *indifference*." Fran keeps one end and gives the other to Gregory. "Notice how close trust stands to her and how far away indifference stands. The next two are *fear* (blue, seven feet) and *hate* (red, six feet) . . . Fran can give these away, or if she doesn't fear anyone, for instance, then she can drop the string—all right, Fran, make your choice."

Fran hands the end of her fear string to Joan. She hesitates a moment and then hands her hate string to Kent Long. So she, Kent, Joan, and I look something like this in the center of the Trip room:

4-foot string—green—trust
8-foot string—yellow—indifference
7-foot string—blue—fear
6-foot string—red—hate

"All right, Barb, your turn. Who're you going to hand the trust string to?"

I quickly hand my trust string to Fran. We've got a two-way thing going now.

"Who do you fear?"

I look toward Kent and hand the blue string to him. He must move a little because now he's holding onto one string six feet long and another seven feet. I look at Mike, "I don't hate nor am I indifferent to anyone." I drop the yellow and red strings.

Mike points to Sean. "All right, boy, let's get going here. Who do you trust?"

Sean hands the string to me; I can barely hold all my trust strings.

"O.K., Sean, who do you hate?"

Sean hands one end to James.

"Indifferent string?"

It goes quickly to Gregory, who's now even further outside our circle.

"Do you have anyone to give the fear string to?"

Sean hands it to Kent. Kent is caught between too many strings. What's he going to do? He can't reach Sean's string.

"All right, Kent, now comes the decision—which of the strings are you going to drop to take Sean's—*if you want it.*"

Kent drops Fran's hate string. He reaches for Sean's fear.

Now it's Matt's turn. He walks toward Fran and me. He tries to hand me his trust string but I'm too bound in by strings to reach it.

"All right, Barbara," Mike says, "you can't move unless you *drop someone's string . . .*"

But I want to keep them all! All their yelling, and all the time, by God, they trust me . . . Who will I drop? Sean. I'm sorry, my handsome friend. I drop his string.

We are a living cat's cradle. Each new person hopelessly entangles our relationships. Until, finally, one way or another, we free ourselves, or strangle.

At last it's Dot's turn. By this time, I have three trust strings; Fran has two, and one fear. It sounds like ice cream cones. Maybe someday we'll walk into a store and ask for one trust, one indifference, and two hates, a la mode. Dot limps toward me.

"Barbara," she says softly. She hands me her trust string. I don't know what to do, I want to take her string, really, but Fran, I can't drop Fran's string. I look at Fran and drop Matt's string. I still can't reach Dot's string.

"Fran!" I cry.

"I don't know what to do, Barb—I can't hold on if you take Dot's string!" She looks around frantically. She drops John's string.

At last everyone's had a turn. Suddenly, I remember that we're not by ourselves, that all those other Trip takers are watching us. Poor Gregory and John. No one fears them; they are almost out the door, we're so indifferent.

"You can drop your strings now," Mike barks. Now I know how a puppet must feel.

A Hoopla album is put on, and everyone gets up to dance. This seamless body—I'm an athlete again, responding instinctively to the air around me, the bouncing ball, the circles of air, the music, the people. Wheel am I, a spinning top—a trust string has spun me out! You know what I'd like to do? I'd like to kneel down and quietly do a somersault behind everyone's back. Just to see the world turn around.

"Vance, Vance!"

"Yeah, Barb?" he smiles.

"Do you know what a Trip is?" I ask.

"What?"

"An adult's way of somersaulting!"

"Great!" We hug.

It must be Sunday morning. So little time . . . Someone produces long loaves of fresh bread. We break it together. Although, for Synanon, it is only a natural expression of fellowship, for me it is the Eucharist, the thanksgiving feast. Afterward, I walk down to the locker room. Propulsion toward extinction—I feel it now. Like a door's swung open and I'm afraid to jump out—what if my parachute doesn't work? What if I'm not ready when the world comes to meet me?

No what ifs, baby, just *act as if* . . . *As if* you're not afraid, jump. But I can't—I'm not ready (will you *ever* be ready?). I'm not sure (who is?); but I don't want to go (nobody wants to at first); who will protect me from the terror of the day? (no one) Will it be worth it? (always, baby—like the man says, life is always an answer unto itself); psalmist! (woman)—yes, *yes*.

# Free time

The night air is eager as I join Mary, Vance, and some others for a walk. The midnight dance is still on my mind. Perhaps, I have enjoyed the sexless swallow too long. Vance had such nice hair, but some time in these past two days, he has gotten his head shaved. A symbolic act, to show that he trusts Synanon.

Glad not to have wasted this free time on sleep. We must come to understand each syllable of the night—sea, empty cars parked on the promenade, lonely homosexuals waiting for a trick, gutted shops, hollow carousel, toothpick pier. We come to the old armory. "This," our blond Shepherd says majestically, "was our old home before we moved to the Del Mar."

She tells us of the great party they had the night they were to move into the Del Mar Club. At midnight, they form a bunny-hop line and dance the few blocks to their new quarters. Everyone is laughing, screaming, hugging; then they walk inside.

The first floor is littered with debris, empty liquor bottles, stale food, cigarette butts.

"So this is the gift, the welcome by the Del Mar people?" Chuck Diedrich bellows. "Ah, wouldn't we love to have a game with the cocksuckers?" There was no time for a game, only work; by noon of the next day, the place is renewed.

I look up at Vance. Renewed. He is Adam; didn't I give him an apple long ago? In the Armory's broken windows there are still traces of sin-flickering bodies. Vance is explaining something to Sidney about the night, about the way the moon touches the waves. My feet are taking longer and longer steps until, suddenly, I'm running. The night air hangs like diamonds. Everything is condensed as I run, pushing, fighting the air, grinding on toward my target—an old telephone pole. On and on, while the air, the pier, the pole, and the buildings bob up and down in the diamond air. I scream, kiss the tree, and the bark hurts my cheek.

In the beginning was the dance, and the dance was the joy of God. I let go of the old telephone pole and rejoin the group. Don't tell them, don't tell how it is:

> alleluia is God and a woman
> dancing on a garden tomb.

# The last eight-hour game

## I.

Words quack in the night. Cardboard dreams are falling off the walls. The world is turning, turning in my stomach. Talk, coffee, and night are flattening out my tongue.

The stupidity of people's lives covers everything like dust. Existence is a last flickering spot of light on a dying T.V. What can Synanon provide but a medicine cabinet filled with bottles?

My body is humped over the side of my chair, my robe hangs on me like a rag, and they go on endlessly, endlessly talking. Words are pasted all over me, jamming my soul.

You know what Synanon is? A thesaurus of sin.

I can't take it any longer. Why don't they turn the Game on me? All through these interminable eight hours, trying to listen, to give. God, let me be able to rise up and say, they tried to touch me but they couldn't; I'm living, see? I'm still Barbara.

When I was little, life was a trampoline. My mother earnestly tried to keep me down. She'd cut switches, use her hands, a brush, use Dad's hands, they even created a spanking board, but my bottom only toughened. I would cower and cry, and genuinely feel compunction, but secretly, I'd overcome them. But now, without open conflict, my mind is limp, my body ragged. I've taken my flipflops on and off a hundred times. After all those showers, so much coffee, and even going swimming, I'm open, all right. These people before me are tight fists.

Mike turns the Game back on the Jewish woman. Her skin is tightening, her eyes bug out. Her nose suddenly seems larger and redder. Tirelessly reviewing her sex escapades before and after marriage—it's no good, Irma, baby, I just don't give a damn. Just stuff bits and pieces of the Kleenex into my fine pink ears. Or drape it over my face so that things will look as fuzzy as they feel.

People come to the feast of sin, but their offering is more words. Endlessly, Mike goes on; how can he do it? Maybe he catches eight hours of sleep or so during our free period, but what a thing to wake up to!

Irma is explaining that she now realizes how she systematically castrated her husband. And her two daughters?

"I've tried to be a good mother," she weeps.

"But have you succeeded?" Mike.

"Well, the older one—such a damn hypochondriac, she bugs me to death. Always hurtin' somewhere, always botherin' me."

"And the other girl?" Mike.

"Oh, she's a gem. It's the first one—every minute beggin' for band-aids, aspirin, iodine."

Always the long tightrope between life and death. Always the waterfall of talk, the tightrope overhead, and the walker. From the edge of a hill one can make out a dog fight down below. Now the pack of dogs begins to swerve after a new victim; imperceptibly, they are changing direction. They are going to turn the Game back to Gregory. I want my turn! My words splatter over my chin like raspberry jam. "I've waited so long. We've been on him before . . . Hell, I hate all you goddamn fools!" What am I saying? Got to wipe away the thick words from my mouth and chin.

"Maybe we're not ready to get on you, Barbara," Mike sneers. "Aren't you being selfish?"

"I'm just tired of listening to all you crybabies," I shout, all the while choking with tears. "Did it ever occur to you that you got yourselves into this mess? That it was your damn selfishness and cruelty that ruined your lives, your marriages, your dime store dreams?" Oh no, they'll take away their trust strings!

"This speech is being made by Sister Asshole," Sean snickers.

*"No good,* Virgin Mary! What fuckin' right do you have to set yourself up?" Mike is breaking a cigarette in two.

"I'm just sick of you all. Nothing's good enough for you. Just hostility and take, take what you can, where you can, hide it in your pocket, and run. I used to think people became fuller as they grew older. I'm twenty-two and have more control and discipline than all of you."

"Discipline? Who gives a damn? Maybe we're lucky and you're not. In the taking and the running we learn something, and you've stopped learning, content to shut yourself up in a nice, clean bathroom. Stay clean in your showers, who needs you?" Sid tosses me away.

"Barbara, did you like your mother?" John leans forward.

"Oh shut up, John. I don't want to be analyzed . . . No, I hate her, strangled her canary neck, put her in a cough-drop box, and sold her to my brother for a nickel." I laugh at his silly face.

"Are you crazy?" Joan is worried.

"No. Disliked my mother as an adolescent but outgrew it," I reply sneeringly, "like I outgrew a lot of things—which is more than I can say for all of you dingbats, crying in your eternally wrung-out towels."

Joan looks at me carefully from across the room. "Is it true, Barbara? . . . What did your mother ever do to you to make you dislike her . . . I always thought somehow that nuns—"

Her voice trails off and I glare at her. "It shows how little you know. Anyway, I was adopted. Mother simply didn't know what to do with me. She works awfully hard; I'm inclined to leisure. She piles up work like clean dinner dishes; I'd rather use paper plates."

"Cut the lecture—get to the point." Mike is bored.

"Watch out," I yell back. "I just might pray to my Catholic God to knock the window down on your inflated Jewish head!" Sean is laughing so hard he almost falls off his tight chair.

"Prejudice?" Irma goads.

"No, damn it. I dated so many Jews my father was convinced I'd marry one . . . I did, sort of." One of my favorite jokes—but it's lost on them.

John picks up the thread. "Your mother? Why did you dislike your mother?"

"Oh, when I was young, she was a nagging machine. I couldn't do anything right. She never seemed to care when I got elected to something in school or did well in a play—just if my room was clean: it never was. She never called me Barbie or honey except if company was there . . . She never even touched me—" I fight against the tears. I won't be like them. It's normal to pull apart from your parents when your bones and flesh are half-formed and each day is a question. At school there was expectation and a bristle of hope. But when I got home, there was my conscience, my blanket, smothering me, trying to catch me doing something wrong.

Someone hands me a Kleenex. Be still; don't try to say anything for a while. As a child, I was Silas Marner piling small grudge upon grudge as if they were pieces of gold. I wouldn't trade my anger, my secret grudges for anything. Later, when I became a Catholic, the idea was to forgive—but it didn't take away the residue of fear. No matter where I was, even after going to boarding school and a year of college, she was still there, still watching for a mistake—"Ah ha! I've caught you, you are a fool." I could never be so engrossed in anything that I wasn't prepared for her shout, "*Barbara* . . . get in here . . . how dare you . . ." One ear directed to life, the other to mother.

But I won't tell them that. Don't give them the satisfaction. I blow my nose. Why let myself be shred apart like Kleenex? I bite the inside of my lip and look up again.

## II.

Fran is looking at me across the room. "Do you ever want sex?"

"Of course. But there are other more important things—I can't explain." My whole body is prickling, like when it falls asleep. I can't find any words, yet this is supposed to be my whole reason for being.

"Fran, move over and sit by Barbara," Mike orders quietly.

Fran gets next to me underneath the mirror.

"Now, Barbara," Mike says, walking toward me, "stand up so that you're facing the mirror . . . I want you to describe yourself . . . What do you see in the mirror?"

All right, I am looking. I smile. What else are you going to do when you have to look at a face like mine? Why not stick my tongue out at the mirror and see if any words are clinging to it? (Probably dirty words, anyway.) Better squelch that impulse, and tell them what I see: "A triangle face that's mostly point. A girl with squinty brown eyes, a bulbous nose, voluptuous lips, nice, even teeth, a slight scar over the upper lip and a tiny pimple on the large chin . . . Oh, the glasses—I see huge nunny glasses."

"Ah hem. Do you like this face?" Mike leans near me.

What is one supposed to say? If I say yes, they'll think I'm crazy or conceited; if I say no, I'm not being open. What I am really proud of is the tongue they can't see. My dentist says I should pickle it, and those who know me best wonder how I can talk without choking to death. I mean, it's a calves' tongue, not a nun's tongue. So I shall say, "Not particularly. But it's only a face." I turn around sharply.

Joan is smiling. "You don't seem to think yourself very pretty."

Now I ask you—no wonder her marriage and her daughter are so screwed up. She won't face facts. I do. The fact is I can't change my face. So I laugh, "How can I?"

"Perhaps you just don't like yourself," Mike comments.

Are they grabbing at shadows! Look fink, I love myself. But myself is under the thin skin of reality. Me is not my face. Me is running next to my skin. Since they won't understand that, I say, "Listen, Mike. I used to hate myself but I outgrew that, too."

"No good! No good! Do you know what I think?" Mike is yelling.

"What?" I am calm again.

"I think you're a bullshitting liar who's not playing straight arrow. You're allowing yourself to be buried alive in the Church to spite your mother and yourself!" Mike is red underneath his beard.

Tinker-toy arguments. I shall smash them with my generous mouth. "Why do ill-informed people always equate the Church and the convent? Religious life is the avant-garde of the Church. And besides, I didn't come from some Catholic ghetto into religious life. My parents aren't Catholics. I've only been a Catholic since I was sixteen. I dated a lot before I entered, and my own free choice led me to the convent. I felt this was the best way to serve others and God." But the words grit my mouth.

"Why can't you serve by marriage? Or is sex a low way of serving the Lord?" Matt inserted.

Great black god crushing his eldridge cleaver hand on me—"Oh shut up!" I explode. "Of course, it isn't. I was just called to do another thing." We speak from different contexts. My words are Bible sentences floating around in a puddle. They can't read me. Got to make them understand! My hands and face are wet from straining. I want to go to the bathroom and flush everything away.

Mike is watching me. "I know how it is, Barbara, to want to do something larger than yourself. That's why I said to hell with the P.R. game in movieland and came here. But don't fool yourself: the Church, convent, call it anything you want, ain't where it's at. They're too far from scruffy people like us. And baby, we're the world."

Talk your cool talk, Mike. He watches me look around the room.

Christ, I pray, Maker of the little people, forgive us now and at the hour of our life. Amen. Open me God; *I got no place to go!*

Mike stands. "All right, Barb. Will you do something for me?" He puts his great hand on my shoulders. "Sure," I whisper.

"Fran? Will you move your chair so that both you and Barbara are facing the mirror?" We move. Something in me is leaning toward Fran. You gave me your trust string. I dropped all the others just to keep yours. Once I saw a frozen cobweb. It was beautiful, yet cold, brittle. I wouldn't touch it for fear it would fall apart in my hands.

"All right, Barbara. I'm going to give you one minute to give Fran the best advice you possibly can." In the mirror, Fran's reddish-brown hair is cut very short in the present Synanon style. She seems gentler and more attractive than she was in that pre-Trip game.

What to say? Too much, and she might fall apart and not be my friend. But I want her to be my friend. "Fran, you're really a great person. You've had a lot of hard knocks but you still have the possibility of growth. You seem cold and distant at first but that's your wall. I like you ever so much! Just keep forgiving yourself and trying. Synanon is growing in you." I stop on one leg, embarrassed.

"All right, Fran," Mike directs, "now you give Barbara advice."

She looks steadily into the mirror. "Barb, I like you. But you've got to make some changes. Stop being ashamed that you are a woman. You are only as attractive as you believe inside. Second, leave the convent. As long as you remain there, you'll have to act like someone you're not. That's my advice: start enjoying your womanhood and leave the convent." She stops. We turn from our glass-moment together.

Mike is standing near us. He motions to the rest of the people. "All right, folks. Who do you think gave the best, the most helpful advice?"

They point to Fran.

"Barbara, how long did you prepare to be a nun, to help people?" Mike says quietly.

"Three years," I answer.

"How long have you been at Synanon, Fran?"

"Seven months," she says quietly.

We are sitting beside each other. "Perhaps it's not such a good preparation for life—the nun-thing." That's all that comes out, because now I'm crying again. But not the heavy tears about mother, for something is growing within me—a residue of midnight.

They are far from me now. I am listening with one ear, hearing them mumble and cry; salvation is here. Well, who needs God, then? Is prostitution a better preparation for giving? I became a Catholic out of necessity for God; I would have died without him. As for becoming a nun, deep in my question-mark bones I felt that nuns were for people, dedicated to them. My pre-convent days were a constant running after God and peace, but not so much for me as for others, those who die stupidly, with a mumble and a grin.

At least that's what I thought: but now, right in front of me, people are being saved by people. Salvation is knowing that you are forgiven; it is then that peace comes. Here at Synanon, without the God-dance or steeple talk, people were offering a kiss of peace. I could even feel the peace coming—but not for me. It's frightening, can I have all this and sex, too? No answer. Better get up now and go to the bathroom for a while.

## III.

When I come back, they are talking to Kent. Every sinew of his great body is angry. He twirls his anger into a tight core of hate, endless circles of it—for his father, for himself, for his wife. Plays games with his anger—it's his way of escape; he can use it as an excuse to cheat on Susie. And escape into a nightly high with the thin, sweet marijuana. Watching him is like watching Vietnam on T.V. This battle can't touch me; I will drink coffee, nibble candy, and be entertained.

Mike abruptly leaves the room, but they keep on Kent until his face blazes. Suddenly, Ted Dibble is with us again, carrying a small silver cane. Kent's red face changes to a slab of frozen meat. Not again, what has he done now? Ted sits in a chair by the door, adjusting his purple robes. He lays the cane carefully on his lap: "Kent Long, come here."

Obediently, Kent gets up and stands in front of Ted. "Sit down." Kent sits on the rug a few feet away from me.

"All right, Kent. I'm your father. Say what you feel to me—" Ted speaks very quietly.

Kent looks up. Hesitates. Then, "All right—Goddamn you, Father! Why did you always have to buy me?"

"I did the best I could, Kent."

"Shit, Dad, why couldn't you just love me for free? Why in the hell—"

"I tried to show I loved you, Kent—it was just my clumsy way of doing it."

Kent puts his hands to his face. "Look, this isn't gonna work. You're not like my father at all. You're too gentle. He'd be rantin' and ravin' if I said this to him."

Ted looks stunned. He raises his voice, and leans over Mark: "Okay, Goddamn it, always suckin' my tit, Kent Long *Junior!* When are you going out on your own, Sonny?"

"That's not true, that's not true! I don't owe you a penny. Sure you gave me a goddamn start, but check the accounts; I've made my own way."

"Always the little liar. You never know when to say thank you, you motherfucker son!"

"*That's not true, Father, that's a lie!*" It's not coming from Kent, but Sean. Sean's almost out of his chair, crying.

Mike: "Go down by your brother, Sean. Sit down by Kent."

Sean, the sleep-walker, sits cross-legged by Kent. Ted stares at him, and quietly says, "I did the best I could, Sean."

"Sure, sure you did, Father—*but why did you always rub my*

*nose in it?* Why?" As Sean leans forward with the force of his words, I am crying with him.

"Did the best I could, the best I know how, Sean."

"Then why did you always hold Jerry up to me? 'See Jerry run? See how smart he is?' I never knew how to live up to him." Sean wipes his nose with his hand.

"I loved you, Sean, it was just my way of wanting you to do better—I always knew you could."

"Goddamn that shit, that's shit! You wouldn't even listen to me—always Jerry, *Jerry!* You never took me to a goddman baseball game—we lived in New York and you never took me to the one place I ever wanted to go, never! *I had to be shipped here before I ever went to a baseball game!*" Sean is bawling now; others are crying, too, but I can't look; I keep watching Kent. How he puts his hand on Sean's trembling knee. Big red Kent draining out anger as his brother dies. What are we going to do? Ted is watching Sean, too.

Finally, he sighs. "I love you, Sean. I had no way of letting you know."

"*Like shit you didn't.* I stole just so's you'd know I was around, that I could do something. Just so you wouldn't compare me to Jerry."

Ted stands and helps Sean up, catching hold of Sean's head and bringing it to his shoulder. Then, abruptly, he leaves the room.

What in the hell can Mike do with this? He turns to Kent and says gently, "Do you see that young guy over there, Kent? So full of anger and hostility he screws life's lid on tight. What are you going to do now, Kent? What are you going to do?"

Kent stands, takes Sean in his burly arms, and they begin to cry.

## IV.

Fran and I are crying quietly; so is Irma. Suddenly, we hear a horrible wailing; where is it coming from? Great rivers of mucus and tears are running down John Barry's face; I've never seen a man cry like that—it's embarrassing.

"Stand up, John," Mike commands. John can barely stand because of the weight of the tears and sorrow.

Mike walks over to us. He helps Irma. "All right, Irma. You be a woman to this poor weak man. You do your woman thing." And she takes John in her arms and they are swaying in his tears.

All she can do is hold him and caress him, and it's not enough. The sound is horrible. I scrunch down in my seat, ashamed; all the fun I've made of this poor alcoholic brain with the fifteen psychiatrists and the constant flow of knowledge that I try to damn and the brain twisters and puzzles that I can never answer. All of it a cover for these tears. Poor John.

Finally, Irma sits down. Mike says, "All right, John, go around the room and find someone to help you." So he begins slowly walking around the room. He looks at each one, hard, for help. Oh, Jesus. Please don't let him come to me. I've been so horrible to him; I won't know what to do. *I don't want to touch him.* He's so wet and ugly. He's coming closer, he's looking at the faces of each person seated on the chairs. I watch him come. Oh God, please. *Please.* And then he is bending toward Fran and me, while I'm digging my nails into her arm. He spreads his thin legs apart and looks at us. Then he holds his hands out to Fran, saying gently, crying, "Fran. You dropped my trust string." Fran jumps up and throws her arms around him and we cry.

Mike. "All right, Barb. Get up and help your friend, Fran." And so I have my arms around Fran and John. And then Fran lets go.

*Don't be afraid, John. I'm your brother, sister, mother, God. Old sad brain man, I'll take care of you. The world is this hug —the quiet and the tears running down our faces. Christmas, Easter, birthdays, intercourse, are only the preparation for this moment. Let it, let it all fall down, John. To be human is to walk in a world of burning center.*

And I feel that I shall never stop hugging him. When his tired hands began to go limp, I pulled them up around me again. Never let this tired, shrugging body go—to think that once I hated him.

Finally, he sits down in the chair beside Mike. By this time he has used so many pieces of Kleenex that Mike laughs. "Look at you, John. You look like a clown with all those Kleenex spots all over you!"

At first, John doesn't understand. He looks about his body hungrily. Then he sees and begins to laugh. For the first time in two months, I'm laughing from deep in my stomach, not from the top layer of my head. Good, real good.

And so we laugh, with John and each other, we laugh because there the proud ass is with multi-colored Kleenex powder puffs and discarded rabbit tails all over his robe. And the room is flooded with tears!

Mike takes John by his hand and leads him to the mirror. John continues to laugh at what he sees in the mirror. Then Mike says, "Do you like what you see?"

*Wham!* John smashes his fist on the mirror. He doesn't speak. Standing on the lip of his world, his body speaks.

"How long since you've cried, John?"

"I—I don't know." John, the brain, becomes the nose, the eyes; his sobs are the rattle of the increased man.

## V.

At last John and Mike sit down. Gregory runs over to sit by Dorothy. He holds her hand gently as if it were a leaf. Kent is taking care of his brother, Sean. Even John is opening! I am light; there is a brightness in things: hello, shadow. Yet, hey, look at Matt—he's all sunk into himself like stone in the back corner of the room. Mike notices, too. Mike's heart is our hearts. He leans back and turns to Matt.

"What's eatin' you, man?"

"I dunno, man. Just feel rotten." He runs more of his story. I just sit there, a shell on the Santa Monica sand, all porous, not thirty anymore. The sea is coming, and I am twenty-two, listening, aware of my womanly parts.

Matt tells how it's downhill for him. As a boy, he'd been in the movies; his Dad had been a minister. Then the never-growing-up, the women, the divorces, the drugs. Synanon. "I still haven't changed, Mike. I'm still searching for the kids I made film with. The old gang. Going out of my mind. I'm still in those comedies."

Maureen is looking at him. "I—" she begins falteringly. She's playing the old lady, afraid to cross the street. Tottering, she says, "I want to say something to Matt."

"Yes," Mike says gently, as if giving her permission.

Maureen gets up, smoothes her robe, and sits by Matt, who sinks deeper into stone. The walls of the room jut out from his body—big, rumpled teddy bear. Maureen puts her fat hand on his knee. He wants her to move it.

"Matt—I realize—what I did to old Sam. Forgot he was whole—human. I'm so sorry, Matt." The crying begins again. But *it isn't fair;* Matt's not old Sam—he's got his own troubles. She's keeping him in the corner, using him. Matt's no scapegoat! Mike looks at me.

"Go over and help them, Barbara."

I go across the room and sit on the other side of Matt. Gray tears are running in wrinkles down Maureen's face. I look at my friend, Matt.

"You've got to mean it, Mo," I warn her, almost savagely. "He'll never be human if you use him. *Do you mean it in your guts?*"

"Yes, yes, forgive me, Matt." She rises, wants to go to him.

"*No good,* Mo," I scream. Then to Matt, "Do you want her to come? Can you—forgive her?" My hand is holding Mo back.

A deep sigh from a black pool, "All right." Mo hugs him. His body doesn't answer. I watch his face. The visible workings of a man trying to answer himself. What can he do? Hit her? Mash her stupid white mistake to bits? What's the use? I can see the thoughts on his face. He does what he must, like the strong man he really is, freely taking the responsibility for forgiveness. He answers her hug.

Mike says quietly, "She needs you, Matt. We all need you, man."

Matt looks up from Mo's shoulder. "You mean that, Mike, you really mean it?"

Mike half stands. Matt hurries to him. "Sure, Matt. *I* need you." Matt puts his arms up to Mike.

"Aw, Mike, I thought you hated me; thought I was no good."

They are crying. Mike wipes his face. All this time, Matt just wanted to know someone cared about him. Just wanted to hear it out loud.

Sitting by Fran now, by the windows. She hands me more Kleenex. Too exhausted to cry anymore, but, oh, don't I feel good! Irma's sitting next to me, and Joan's across from us: It's like a game of musical chairs, crying chairs.

"*Wow wee!*" Mike lets out a kid's sigh. "Hey, Matt, sing us a song, won't ya?"

Matt stands again and begins to sing a beautiful hymn in his mellow voice. All I can hear is that it's something about Christ. Christ.

## VI.

I let go of the kite. Free. What's important is this circle of people and the skin freshening, prickling against dry bones. Across from me is Joan; her skin is puffy and turning a little gray around the edges. She looks like a marshmallow toasting.

"Mike?" she asks in her whiny voice.

"Yeah?" All this is too much for him now. He is lighting a cigarette and trying to stretch out his legs. There, hairy legs, breathe again. Peace is in this room but not in Joan. We've been on this bus so long. We've struggled and come to greet one another; now we don't yell. I'm happy in small things. Fran? I want to say something to Fran but I don't yet know quite what. Vance? Will I see Vance during the break? Oh, but let this go on. Always the long tightrope between yes and no. I want to spread my arms apart and hoopla. Good, *good.*

"Mike, there is something I want to say." I look again at sweet, puffy Joan.

"Shoot, Joan," Mike says. He takes his legs off the small table.

"I told you before that I loved my daughter. That I always cared for her and that the only time I even thought about hurting her was when she took that overdose . . . *Not true!* I suppose

I hated her before in little hates. Used to leave her alone for long periods of time, didn't want to be bothered. I never touched her. I can't remember ever kissing her . . . I wasn't a good mother. I know that now." She's crying; wiping her red nose on a pink Kleenex. "I—I want to say I'm sorry."

Mike leaves his chair. He sits down on the rug in front of her, his back to Fran and me. Very gently, so I can barely hear him, he says, "Do you really want to, Joan?"

"Yes, Mike." She wipes her eyes.

"You have to *really* want to. It's not just yourself you have to worry about. Her—I don't think she's ready, Joan—" Still he speaks gently.

I'm looking at Fran. She's crying. Horrible, but somehow, it's right; it has to come. I put my hand on her shoulder, wondering what to say. My hand presses into her shoulder: don't be afraid, Fran, I'm here. I love you, don't ever be afraid. And Joan is walking toward us. I am so frightened for Fran, but what is there to do? Oh, God.

Mike sits down in his own chair. He's to the left of us. "Stand in front of both of the girls, Joan," he says quietly.

She is standing in front of both of us but she's looking at Fran. My hand is getting tighter and tighter on Fran's shoulder; she is crying harder and harder. Please don't hurt her, Joan, please. Joan leans toward Fran and whispers, "I'm sorry, Fran. Really, I'm so sorry." Fran's face is covered by one hand; the other is waving at flies. "No, no," Fran answers. I am answering, crying, too.

Joan won't let up. "I'm sorry, Fran. *Please* forgive me."

Mike breaks in, "No, Joan—you're talking to the wrong girl."

But Joan keeps on, "Please, Fran. Look at me, I'm sorry."

And again, Mike interrupts quietly, "No, Joan—the wrong girl."

Joan must be looking up but I can't see anything now. "What?" she says.

"*Barbara*, Joan—she's the one." Gently, the sky is falling down. Suddenly she's on her knees before me and I don't know what to do. All I can give is tears. All the times—the ugly wart-heap times—are pouring out of my eyes, nose, and mouth. "Barbara—" I can't look up.

"Barbara?" She pulls my chin up with the question. "Barbara, I'm sorry." It is a gentle statement.

*"You're not sorry,"* I choke.

"I am, Barbara, I truly am." She is strong now and gentle, for the rain is falling.

"No, no—I can't forgive you—*never!*" The words bang out like bullets.

"Please, Barbara. I'm sorry." Gently, gently, the sky is falling down.

"It's too late. I'm grown now. I don't need you. I've lived all my life without your apologies." Then slowly, through the slug of tears and anger, I hear Mike speaking. I cock my head a little to hear.

*"Harden not your hearts as you did in Meriba."*

It is the Jew psalming the Christian. Let me pull myself above the weight of my anger—but I can't, I can't! Inside the envelope of my body, there is fire, uncontainable. "I can't forgive; it's too late! Where were you when I needed the apologies?" I throw it in her marshmallow face.

*"How many times shall I forgive my brother?*
*Seven times? . . . No, Peter, seventy times,"*

Mike chants softly.

Mike is saying something, but I can't put out the fire. Like I'm gripping at a string inside that has never been gripped—can't get at it. Then: "Have you ever asked your daughter's forgiveness? Have you ever tried to say, I'm sorry—*without* words?" Because I'm remembering when I was nineteen and working all summer, taking a day off and going to the beach to spend six or seven hours in the sun. Back to work the next day, but so sick—the heat is working its way under the crust of my skin. I can't sit down or rest my cheek on a cool wall; the heat keeps coiling around my body and any touch is like flame touching flame. Maimed, I limp home, barely pausing to release the door. I'm entering my tomb with lips cracked and enlarging; every step I take runs up my ankles and twists around my calves. I can't bend my knees; the hollows are screaming. Impossible to move, or lie down, or sit.

Out of nowhere, my mother enters my room. I hadn't seen her, I hadn't asked her to come, but she's here, some E.S.P. of pain has told her. Something cool, she is putting something cool behind my knees; she is spreading something fresh upon my body. My face is ashes; she is putting out the fire. I begin to cry. And inexplicably, as light travels to light, as understanding travels from a limp child to a mother, she's crying, too. Flame touching flame. In the center of the tears and the fire, my mother and I are holding each other and crying. There is no room for small apologies. And I remember, as Joan says, "No, but I will ask her soon. I'll go right down to San Diego and tell her." She doesn't understand yet. It's all been said. But my mother understands, so I answer, "All right, Joan, I know. I know that you're sorry." And so we cry, we hug each other, for the sky is falling down.

At last, shipwrecked, but safe on the beach, I lean back. Irma, sitting next to me, has her face in her hands. I go to her, pull her to me.

She whispers in the shell of my ear, "What you said, what you said—my daughter," and I understand. So I answer her, "Don't—don't ever not show her your love. When you want to shut her down, because—she's a bother—always doing things wrong—just remember me—Barbara."

## VII.

We are little rows of kisses, pennies in a charity card. But two places are empty.

Synanon is a megaphone, a shape, a form, for the human voice. It gives people somewhere to yell. But more important, it has the resources to do something with anger.

We beat each other up in our fearful, shaky, terrifying way. Cutting each other up with words. Pounding into the stomach, the ears with words. Rope-burning the back of our neck and arms with words. But it isn't words that destroy us, but the everyday silences. The silences that hang all over our body and mind like skin cancer, working in us relentlessly, corroding everything that is essential to life. God, like man, does not come to us in the taut silences, but in the Word; and we to each other in words.

Some people say they don't object to the anger as such, but are outraged at the way a sensitivity game manipulates people's emotions. I can't speak for everyone, but there are certainly many for whom this is damn good. People like John—impossible to cure by words. How do you tell someone to *live?* Do you whisper it in his ear? Write it on his mirror? Sing it on the radio of his mind? You can't tell someone how to *feel* life; he has to reach out his hands and do it himself. But, in some degree, you can direct his hands. You can help him, perhaps cure him by your free feeling of it, near him, heart beating against heart.

Take James and Sidney—two ice cubes left in a melted tray, the two places still empty in the charity card.

James had listened, struggled through the entire Trip, but ever since the pre-Trip introduction to him, Mike hadn't made contact. And now it was as if a great tidal wave had gone past him. He stood at the edge of our circle, his long red moustache twitching, tugging the hems of our robes, crying, "Let me in!"

What can we do for him? Unlike John, he has cried enough. Floated through all these hours together in his tears. But all he wants to do is cry some more, with our attention riveted upon each tiny tear dribbling down his face; to hell with him! How can we help? Surely not words again, not tears.

Then there's Sidney. He has been with us all these hours, without ever being mentioned. He's made no connection in my mind or heart. He's typical, that's all. The typical Synanon bald head with traces of sideburns to let you know he's still with it. One can see the traces, even in his robe, of mod clothes—the Nehru jacket, bell bottoms, and, of course, a paisley scarf. He told us once that he wasn't gay. He lives with a Negro girl whom he plans to marry soon. Besides working as a P.R. man, he has produced one film and is looking for a market for others. A twenty-four-year-old ice cube. Why has he come? Is it just that Synanon and drugs are "in"?

If you don't develop some depth, a sense of tragedy in life, no one can give it to you. It can't be pinned, stapled, or paper-clipped into your being. If life hasn't reached its hands deep inside, until your whole body is sick and reeling with it, and you cannot breathe for the brass taste of it, then nobody can reach you. You'll skate on your little ice cube all the days of your life.

Two cavities in a mouthful of firm, white teeth. James, the rabbit, moving his whiskers eagerly. Sidney, the ice cube, hands behind his back, moving his feet listlessly.

"Do you want to cry, Sid?" Mike asks.

"Yes—but I can't. Nothing has touched me—at least not for long." Sid runs his hand over the fuzz of his head.

"I'm all cried out . . . I just can't cry again," James whimpers.

Mike stands up. "All right, James," he sighs. "Will you stand up in the middle of the room?"

James stands in the middle of us like a rabbit surrounded by hunters. Now his body whimpers. Alone, alone in the midst of us.

"Close your eyes, James."

Mike puts his hands on Jamie's eyes. Then James covers them with his own hands. Mike motions for Fran. She stands near Mike, and he takes her hands and places them on Jamie's shoulders. Then he calls Sid and puts his hands on Jamie's left side. Then Mo, to put her hands on the other side. Then Mike calls me. He motions with his hands for me to kneel on the floor. I immediately obey, not yet understanding.

"Hold his feet." He mouths the words.

From that moment on, all I know is holding Jamie's feet. All the care that I am as a woman is bent on those small, red feet. Others have been called to lay their hands upon James but I can't see them. All I know is Jamie's feet, lifting a little with the weight of their hands. I can understand everything in his feet—the fear, the sighing, the weight of them on his tiny body.

I am enveloped in bodies as James is. But free of their pressure, only knowing the slight rocking of his feet.

Mike goads, "Press harder." I feel the press in Jamie's feet. I tell him not to be afraid. Somewhere Matt begins to sing, "He's Got the Whole World in His Hands . . ." I bend my whole body over those little feet and my head rests upon them.

We all press harder. I am surrounded by a tepee of people, leaning toward James, all saying quiet, wordless things with the weight of their hands.

So this, my Father, is what Sean and I were preparing so many hours ago. Suddenly, it becomes clear why Christ chose to wash the apostle's feet. I can't be Peter now. Joyfully, I cradle Jamie's feet in my tired hands. Is that crying above me? Oh, let me look up, let me join them; I want to see what's going on. Is that movement the brushing of robes? Down here I'll never see what's happening. Oh, gentle God, isn't this my place, sister to James, caring for his feet? *I belong here.* No other place but the place forgotten, caring for the least of my brothers, James. There is a flower growing within me.

Suddenly an avalanche of joy and tears, James falling upon me, embracing and tears. Just he and I. Everyone has gone. I hold him in my arms.

And there is Sidney, open, embracing, caring.

When at last I stand, Matt, Mo, and Fran are rocking and swaying as they sing,

"In the morning, in the morning
Lord you rose, Lord you grew
In the morning, in the morning
Lord you rose, Lord you grew
And you made us free
And we are free,
Alleluia, Alleluia, all for thee."

When it was time to go, they had to drag us apart. How we had fought to come together. In some forty-four hours, we had compressed a lifetime of fumbling.

When I am old and my nude bones quiver in the frail air, let me remember this: how once I knew that we are separated only by a thin skin from resurrection.

"What must I do to gain life?" the young man asked Him. He answered in Camus' words, "Yield to the world, feel the weight of flesh and bones."

# *Last free time*

Meeting Mary in the locker room, I can't contain myself: "Oh, Mary, it was so beautiful!" We lean together for a moment.

"I know, Barb," she answers. "I can't wait to tell you how it was . . . Ted's such a great guy."

"He came to your Game, too?"

"Yes, I guess our Game leader asked him to. He's such a good man, Barb; I really love him."

"Don't limit it, Mary!" Our arms are gently around each other.

We decide to venture our first steam bath in the Spa. To think I was too frightened to take one before! As we go down the steps, however, Mary turns to me with a gesture of caution.

"Okay, Barb. You watch the door. Knock if anyone comes."

"Mary!" I laugh. "You mean to tell me you're afraid of a bunch of nude women? Shame!"

She giggles. "Who cares about nude women? I just don't like to be nude in front of them." It still doesn't make much sense, but she smiles reassuringly: "I mean, I'm just not used to it. Remember, in the Novitiate, when we had to dress under our bathrobes?" So Mary takes a shower, wraps herself thoroughly in a towel, and zips into the Spa looking like a hot dog—while I have to watch the door.

Afterward, we go upstairs to the big dining room. Everyone in the Trip is crowded into a few tables. People from my Game call me over. I sit down by Fran, Sean, and Mike. We are tired of words and the food is good.

After dinner, we go back to the main Trip room. Ted is smiling. "Would everyone please stand in a large circle." We obey quickly. "All right," he continues, "this is the last part of your Trip. It is the end of what we hope was one of the greatest experiences of your life. But if you haven't opened yourself—if you've remained closed, particularly in the last eight-hour game—my heart goes out to you, for you have gained nothing and the Trip is lost for you." He looks around the room. "Now, there were a few requests made to me during the midnight hour—I'm ready to answer them now."

A very thin woman who worked with me at the School came forward. "Ted—all I want—may my cousin please be allowed to come to Synanon?"

Ted takes her face in his hands and answers simply, "Sure, honey, he may come."

Then he looks over toward my side of the circle. "All right, Barbara." What's he talking about? All right for what?

He seems to be waiting for me. "All right, Barbara," he says again. "I promised you a family at Synanon. You may choose those members of your family now." What family? When did I ask for a family? I don't remember, the dream—Mo's and Jamie's hands—I could use a family here. And Vance. I walk out toward Ted. I look at each face in the circle.

"Matt—I'd like Matt to be my dad." Fine, fine man.

Matt looks down at the rug. He takes my hands and then kisses me as he comes forward.

I'm searching . . . "Joan—will you be my mother?"

She smiles delightedly, "Of course, Barbara." She comes forward and takes Matt's hand.

"Fran is my sister." Fran hugs me.

"And Vance, my brother." But there are other voices in me saying other things.

Matt, Joan, Fran, and Vance go back to the side of the circle with me. I now have my own cat's cradle, made by invisible trust strings. There are other reunions until finally it is Kent Long's turn.

He takes Susie by the hand and comes out to the center.

"I just want to let all of you know, I'm sorry about all that I've done—really sorry."

Ted looks at him suspiciously. "You really care about coming back to Synanon, Kent?"

"Yes, Ted . . . I've never cared about anything so much in my life," Kent answers quietly. There are beads of perspiration on his bald head. "Why, Kent?" Ted asks.

"Because I'm sick of being a coward and I want to be a man . . . I need Synanon to help me go straight."

Ted puts his arm around Kent. "We all need Synanon, Kent."

And then it was time to go and none of us wanted to leave each other . . . The Shepherds tell us to make a huge line and hold each other's hands; we were to go down to the main floor. As I hold onto John's and Fran's hands, I feel proud. Will they see the difference?

The Hoopla is playing downstairs. I push against John; "Let's get going," my feet and body keep saying. They almost tear my arms off as the great snake line of people begins to move. The main floor of the Club is packed with people. First we dance the Hoopla by ourselves and then everyone joins us. We hug everyone in sight. I see Saba.

"Saba! Saba!" I run to him. "You were right—thank you—how glad I am that I came!"

He's laughing. "We'll talk about it soon, Barb."

I see Nina, Al, Dede. "I'm free." I throw myself in Dede's arms. "It was so great—above all, the hand touch and the sculpture . . . I felt so transparent!"

The crush is tremendous. I keep hugging until my arms won't move anymore. Everyone is here. Mel, Mannie, Ray—all the kids. I pick Nicky up and almost smother Kenny.

Finally, I close the door leading down to the locker rooms. "Hey, Barb." It's Kent.

"Hi!" I answer. He's a larger man now; I'm even beginning to like his moustache.

"Listen, whatever happens—whatever you decide, let's keep in touch." He has his arm protectively around Susie. "You'll come and have dinner with Susie and me, won't you, Sister?"

"Gladly," I smile and walk on.

But it's all over. I'm back where I started; again, that metallic sound, the scratching, banging of people's lockers. "Sister—"

I turn; it's Dot. "I just want you to know—wherever you go—whatever decision you make, I wish you the best of luck, you're a beautiful person."

I look at her—what decision? As if you know anything about me, lame-woman. Am I supposed to change my life because thirteen people decide for me? I smile at her, "Thanks, Dot. I admire your courage, too." I slam my locker door.

It's all over. I am aware, stiffly, that my skirt is too short.

# 3.

# coming out of the cave

*"Union of the weakest develops strength*
*Not Wisdom. Can all men, together, avenge*
*One of the leaves that have fallen in autumn?*
*But the wise man avenges by building his city in snow."*

W. Stevens, *L*

# John's puzzle

The shower finds me in one of my watusi-girl moods. God, it's been a long time since I've sung there! My voice never sounds so good as when it's surrounded by a hundred gallons of water. Oh well, all of us are frustrated. Thoughts and images rush out of my head as if my forehead were a billboard and all these ugly tom-thoughts were sliding down . . . Been thinking lots since my trip—little short phrases like, "she's the kind of person who's always going around saying, I'm a violin in a world of whiners!" Been thinking that I'm condemned to my own sensitivity and conscience.

It's lonely riding to school in the jitney; but I can't wait to get there. The best time at the beach is early morning, when the ocean collapses against ocean sand. I know it'll be better. If Synanon can completely tear apart twenty-four hours and combine moments in a new way, perhaps I can do it with my own schedule, with my own self. The world sways with infinite possibilities.

Children's voices collide on the beach in front of the School. Nicky runs up: "Hey, Sither, did you like your Trip? Can we play mifts again? I like killing the turtle!"

"You're not supposed to call her Sister!" Susie says quickly.

I look at her. "Why not?"

"Al says you're just like anybody else. We don't call anybody else Miss or Mister, so you're not supposed to be called Sister."

I laugh.

"Look, Sither—Barbara!" I follow Nicky's hand. A small boy's ice cream cone has thudded upon the beach promenade. He is inconsolable. His parents are dragging him away, but his sorrow has given him superhuman strength. They drag one way and he shrilly pulls the other way. Mother! Surely his ice cream cone can be salvaged. The hot sun bubbles its vanilla coolness into the asphalt. Each of us has his own ice cream cone tragedy, but ain't I free, ain't I me? For once, I am happy.

Going up the steps to my workshop, I think of John. How he takes a piece of paper with his precise hands and makes up impossible puzzles for me. Once he even tried to explain how a computer works.

"But, John dear, really, I—I'm not much for computers"—which is to say the least, having barely passed addition, but John is not stopped, his intellectual ecstasy has given him fangs.

"Really, Barbara, this computer is very easy to comprehend—Each of these cylindrical surfaces," he drones on, "is equivalent to the square root—"

But because of the Trip I understand him and love him. Someone who created his life around him on the strength of his mind, not realizing the possibility of his heart. It would be great to get to know him, not as computer, but man.

"How do you feel?" I ask as I sit down.

"Marvelous! I was just trying to work out a scenario for my new play," he says, arranging scraps of paper precisely.

"Play? About what?"

"About fourteen people locked in one room who discover each other."

I smile. "Sounds vaguely familiar—but I wouldn't write it if I were you."

"Why not?"

"Because life is cheapened when you set it down that way. Besides, even if you were Shakespeare you couldn't say it as it was. How it was for us." I put my arm lightly in his.

"It was good, that's all I know," he answers quietly. "And if I could write it, what a fantastic play it would make!"

"Must we always preserve things in a show-off way? Can't we just feel them in our guts?"

"Yes, feel them deeply. My, Barbara, you're certainly picking up the Synanon lingo."

"Well, I've got this tape inside me, see . . . When I'm home with the Irish, I say, 'Would you ever do this for me?' and I have Erin go Brau and little shillelaghs in my voice. When I'm with New Yorkers, I pull out my elongated *o*'s and *a*'s, saying things like 'New Yoork,' etc., and when I'm here, it's Synanonese, I say 'split,' 'hangout,' spiced with a little—"

"Unmentionable phrases. But what will you do when you go home?"

I looked at him a moment. "I—I really don't know, John. The Trip . . . I guess I was changing before, but I didn't realize . . . Can't you just see me, John? Standing majestically in front of my fifth-graders, and barking out, 'if you assholes don't understand this math problem . . .' " I make a movement with my hand.

He claps his hands with laughter, "Good, good!"

"Hey, John—" I watch him light another cigarette. "Do you really think Fran gave the best advice?"

"When?"

"When we were both looking in the mirror?"

"Well, Barbara, if you noticed, and I'm sure you did, Mike Kaiser took particular pains with Fran."

"How do you mean?"

"I mean that he went out of his way to build her up, to let her see that she was worth something . . ."

"Then it wasn't true? You mean, I gave the best advice?"

He flicked his cigarette. "Not at all, dear. Fran didn't need Mike's help by then. She gave, unequivocably, I would say, the best advice."

"But how? All she said, really, was for me to leave the convent!"

He laughs. "Well? Need I say more?"

"But that's what everyone's been saying since I've come to this damn place. Anyway, what makes her advice so special?"

"One always has illusions about prostitutes. What do some poets call them—'love artists'? Those whose profession is love. It seems to me that besides her experiences, she was about the same age as you, and she had had the same background as you, at least until her fifteenth year, so perhaps her advice would strike pretty close."

"I don't know . . . I like Fran a lot, but why does everyone always think that nuns are so far away from life?"

"Isn't it obvious to you?"

"Well, I mean—*that's* not everything and I do feel life a lot."

"My dear Barbara, feeling and living are very different. It's the difference between a virgin and a woman."

I stand up. "Oh, come off it, John. A virgin's a woman, you know that. You don't have to—'fuck'—to be a woman."

"Really?" he smiles. "In whose opinion?"

"What do you mean?"

"Face it, Barbara dear. Virginity's not only unfashionable, but pointless."

"What's so pointless about being—well, it's a bad word, but, pure?"

"Delusions of grandeur."

"But how do you know?"

"Good God, girl, I'm a man, aren't I?"

I sit down again. "All right, maybe it is passé, but don't some men want the gift?"

"Gift? Good God, virginity's just a flesh-fold. How little you know."

"Very funny . . . What do you mean?" I inch forward in my chair.

"A man today doesn't want to marry a virgin. That's an obsolete wives' tale. Do you have any idea what it is to make love?"

Boney old slob. "Of course I do!" I gulp quietly to myself.

"Obviously you do not, my dear," he dances his arms in the air. "Love—love-making's an art—a man does not want a beginner, Barbara."

"But what of respect and discipline? How does a husband know you won't cheat?"

"Dear Barbara, he's never sure. But that's not the point. Have you ever loved?"

"How do you mean?"

"Fallen veil over orthopedic shoes in love?" He put out his cigarette.

"No," I concede. "Haven't had too many opportunities." I stand up again; don't want to talk about it anymore.

John puts his hand on my shoulder. "I consider that the greatest loss, my dear—the greatest loss."

Like I said, John's always setting up impossible puzzles for me to figure out.

# A violin in a world of whiners

I dreamed I went down to the Synanon Club and sighed outside its doors.

"Why, yes, Sister, you can become a beautiful people, too," the woman said. "All you need is fake eyelashes . . . contacts . . . caps for your teeth . . . hmm, probably a brown wig would look best, until you can get a decent dye job. Fine—now your figure. Take these pills. No, that will take too long. Ah! Use this padding and that girdle. Nice. Let's see, your waist is too low, wear your clothes here. Yes, I know it's uncomfortable, but . . . But your legs, what are we going to do with your legs, Sister?"

"I don't know. That's why I wore a long habit," I answered her.

Again and again, like a wheel stuck in mud, I revolve with the sadness of things. Beyond the apartment window, there is Pico Boulevard, a dark tunnel of black and brown. A suburb of alleys, garbage cans, blacks with black glasses and naturals, browns with brown grease shining on the forehead, and dogs yelping. Of course, dogs yelp anywhere, even in Palos Verdes, but it's different on Pico Boulevard. One yelp is from a steel curl of guts, the other is a well-fed burp.

Mary is resting on the sofa. "Is it really true?" I ask. "Did we really enter the convent to cut problems down to size? So that we wouldn't have to worry about our looks or our ability to compete? To have everything snipped down to the proper perspective—postage-stamp size, on a letter sent to God?"

"I just don't know, Barbara. Synanon's two things for me—one, it's an answer to problems."

"Yes, far more effective than Settlement half-way houses or correctional institutes."

"But for me, although it's an answer to problems (not necessarily my own), it's also an introduction to them. I don't know, Barbara, ever since the Trip, I'm so ambivalent . . ." She takes a sip from her coke.

"Not me, baby—like, I'm beginning to feel like Barbara

again, like I don't know—even if I have piano stool legs, what's me's great!" I jump around in my chair.

"That's not what I mean." Her long lashes close over her face. ". . . I saw so much during the Trip, I saw people open and change right before me."

"Me, too, particularly John Barry. Mary, he was—"

"Shut up a minute, Barbara! I've got to tell you something, but you don't give me a chance." She nervously lights a cigarette.

"Okay, Mary, I'm sorry."

She puts one hand to my face. "No, Barb, don't be sorry, I—something happened during the Trip. I can't stop thinking about it."

My throat's dry, but I don't want to interrupt her.

"It was our last eight-hour Game, the end of it. There was a young girl with us, about our age, who had recently been separated from her husband. Hated him, Barb, but most of all she hated the baby—because he looked so much like the husband and she couldn't stand to have him around reminding her constantly of the man she despised." She takes a drag off the cigarette.

"How horrible."

"Yes. Well, I could see she wanted to tell us something. She had begun sentences all through the Trip without ever finishing them. You know, how the last part of the Trip was—we were all so happy and really free. Ted was with us and he had just finished talking to me. Then suddenly, the young girl turned very pale—"

"Yeah?"

"And said, 'I've got to tell you,' and everybody stops and just looks at her. She's holding onto both sides of her chair and looks like she's going to faint. 'I hated him so much,' she says.

" 'Who?' Ted asks.

" 'My husband. I hated the child. It—it was lying there, sleeping. I . . . It was almost time to come down.'

" 'Where? Come where?' Ted says.

" 'Down here—to the Trip. I hated it so much. I took the blanket,' and she makes a movement with her hands as if she had the blanket, 'and I put it over his head and I kept pressing and pressing, and he stopped crying—he didn't cry again.' Then she looks at us hard. 'I *killed* it,' she screams, 'I killed my baby!' "

"God! Mary!" I put my arms around her. "What did you do? What did you do?"

"What could we do? We just looked at her crying. Finally, Ted said very softly, 'What do you want?'

"She looked up at us, her face smeared with tears. 'Please . . . I . . . I'm so sorry,' she said."

"What did Ted do?"

"He did the only thing he could do, Barbara. He got up and took her into his arms and he said, 'I forgive you,' and she looked at us—and all of us, simultaneously, got up and ran to her. It was beautiful, somehow, but terrifying . . ."

"So, you like this Vance?" She had washed her face and was in a chair now.

"I don't know, Mary. I'm so unused to all this . . . Do you know what John asked me, he asked me if I'd ever loved."

"What did you answer?"

"What else? You know, it's the funniest thing . . . Once I gave a poetry reading for a group of Beverly Hills High School students who were on retreat. I read my little poem with the long title—"

"How does it go?"

"The Ecstasy Passed From One to Another

Is no more lasting
Than wind will last upon a leaf—
But oh, how it changes the leaf as it passes."

"And they liked it very much, except this one young guy sitting by his girl. He asked me to say it again, so I did, and then he just looked at me quietly and said, 'If you only knew, Sister . . .' And you know, Mary, he's right, I don't know, and it scares me!" I put my face in my hands.

"What? What scares you?" She comes over to me.

"The whole crappy thing . . . Damn it, Mary, the worst feeling for a woman is this waiting. Hand and heart tied; one can't call or write him or go to see him. He's got to do it first. After the Trip he just left. The worst sound for a woman is 'I'll be busy the next few days, but I'll call you next week.' You know he won't call because there will be a thousand new strings that will keep him away from your life. And then the waiting; I can't stand it. It's like I'm in the Novitiate again, waiting to get into community to teach and serve. Maybe he's my new Novitiate."

"But it's worth it, Barb, infinitely—"

"How do you know?"

"Because, what a man is—I don't know, Barb, I can't say it like you—but I felt it in the tragedy of that young girl. I would have taken her child. If she'd only known." She looks out the window.

"Know something, Mary? I had the funniest experience during the Trip."

She glances over at me. "Yes?"

"I've always liked being a woman. I mean, liked some of the things but hated the dependence. Then suddenly—you're going to laugh, when I tell you."

"I'll not laugh."

"Well, I was sitting in the Club lounge during one of the Free Times during the Trip and I was watching some men talk, and suddenly," I swallowed, "suddenly I wondered what it was like to have genitals. I mean, I felt, in their absence, what I was—enclosed, deep—"

"Yes," she agreed thoughtfully.

It was late already.

"Oh, Mary, how brief our bodies be! We can't let one day go by without a fine hair growing all over us. No freedom from our needs."

She laughs. "How right you are!"

"What I'm saying is, I used to see things like, only from my mind . . . *I* did the probing with my mind ticking, clicking, going round." I touch my head. "What, what will happen to me if I allow myself to be probed?"

"I don't know . . . Gosh, Barb, what's happening to us? Where are we going?"

"I don't know, Mary . . . What day shall we drink? What night shall we need?"

# Let it all hang out

"But, Mary," I cry, "there is nothing I can do; with my face, even hair spray won't help."

"You could always rat it, you know." She's laughing.

"Very funny." I look in the mirror. "But thanks for cutting my hair."

As soon as I get into the jitney to ride to the School, people notice my hair. I guess it was conspicuously long. But it couldn't be cut so easily in the beginning. Now, with a new sense of Synanon's possibilities—it seems the least one can do.

Arriving at the School, I'm told that Dede wants me in the children's Stew. It seems funny to hear "Dede wants you," instead of Al. Wonder how Al's doing as a Director; haven't seen him since my Trip.

Dede puts a seat near him in the circle. Vicki is sitting near me. There seems to be an unusual number of adults in the Stew; even Father Mike's here.

"Well, Barb, it's good to see you—I wanted you to join us this morning to tell us about your Trip. Was it good?" Dede smiles.

"It was *the* most liberating experience of my life," I reply excitedly. The children look at us with bored expressions.

Dede ignores them. "What did you like best?"

"Gosh, Dede—I loved everything, really, but—probably, the hand touch and the last eight-hour game."

"Yes. But what about—what did you call it, the night you got off the Trip—what did you do on the sand?" he looks at me kindly.

"The sculpturing, you mean?"

"Yes, you seemed to enjoy that so much," Dede leans forward.

"Why, Barb?" Vicki moves a little in her chair.

"Well, Vicki, it was the first time that I've consciously enjoyed the use of my body. During the Trip, I didn't feel—" I look nervously around the Stew room, "so awkward."

"Come on, Dede!" one of the kids yells. "We've got some indictments against people—you said this wouldn't take long."

"Yeah, Dede, this is a bore," a blond girl exclaims.

Dede looks hard at the kid who started it. "Listen, asshole; the Stew is a learning experience. It goes both ways. Sometimes we adults listen to you, sometimes you listen to us! Today you're going to learn by shutting your trap. Barbara just might have some worthwhile information to share with us." He turns back to me. "There's one thing, Barb, that I've always wanted to ask you, and now that I'm running the Stew, I have a chance. I know how I felt as a minister coming to Synanon to teach the "heathens and I wonder how it was with you. Frankly, the one thing that really shocked me was the language." He chuckles to himself. "Sounds crazy, because I'd been in the Navy, but it really upset me. I can't tell you how I felt the first time I heard 'motherfucker'!" He slaps his hand on his forehead.

I smile. "Gee, at first it bugged me, Dede, but then—well, I just got used to it."

Dede looks abashed. "Are you serious? Maybe I'm just pushing the old Wasp heritage on you. The Protestant no-drink, no-swear dictum—but, whew!" He slaps his forehead again. Then with one eye partially covered, he says, "Didn't even a little cocksucker get a rise out of you . . . It used to embarrass the hell out of me!" Dede went on. "Here I was raised in a strict Protestant background, my Dad was a dedicated minister; the first time I heard that expression in the Navy, I would automatically say a prayer."

"Gee, you could have been president of a Holy Name Society," I mutter.

"Well, yes," he laughs, "but Barbara, you certainly have come from a scarier background than I." He hitches his pants up and moves in the chair.

"Ye-es," I begin dubiously.

Vicki smiles very wisely at me. "Barb, maybe it wasn't *that* word that bothered you . . . Seriously, which words used in the Game upset you?"

Vicki's pretty smart, she's on to something. But one word? Maybe some phrase that really bothers me? "Well, to tell you the truth, Vicki, there *is* one phrase that really gets me," I falter.

Even the kids are interested. Dede smiles, "Which one? We use so many!"

Very slowly, I let it roll. "I absolutely despise the phrase 'let it all hang out.' "

Dede claps his forehead with laughter. " 'Let it all hang out!' I don't believe it. It's so harmless—what about 'fuck' . . . ? 'asshole' . . . ? Are you sure that's the one?"

"Wait a minute, Dede," Vicki says quickly. "I think I understand what Barbara is getting at. That phrase *is* harmless, in itself, isn't it, Sister?"

"Yes. I guess so," I fidget in my chair.

"But you visualize something by it, don't you?" she continues.

Dede snaps his fingers. "You mean it doesn't mean to dump your guts out, as it does to us? It has some sort of sexual connotation—is that what you're getting at, Vicki?"

She nods.

"You know," I say admiringly, "Vicki caught my meaning from the very first, but you missed it, Dede. Maybe it's because as a woman she caught the meaning the phrase would have for another woman—"

"Very true, Barb," Dede leans back in his chair thoughtfully. "But I'm more and more struck by the change the Trip has wrought in you. You even speak differently; you're freer, more your own age."

Vicki lights another cigarette. "But the Trip meant more that that for you, Barbara, didn't it? A sexual awakening of some sort?"

She is waiting for my answer and I feel uncomfortable, probably because Father Mike is in the room. The last representative of my past. "Yes, I guess you're right, Vicki." Mike doesn't seem to be paying any special attention; why should I mind saying this in front of him? "But I suppose the Trip made me aware of the wonder of being a man."

Dede looks puzzled. "Do you mean man in general or particular?"

Vicki stops him. "I don't think the kids understand that, Dede."

So Dede goes to the board and writes: "Man: *General* means that we're all a part of the same species or group, called man;

*particular* can mean two things, a specific man, say, Joe, or, man as a particular sex." A few kids nod their heads. Dede sits down. "Okay, Barb."

"I suppose I mean both meanings of particular . . . For the first time, God, I saw what a man could do! Like I've lived with women so long I'd forgotten a guy can be just as compassionate and sensitive as any woman. Take Mike Kaiser—he's beautiful; I've never seen such a perceptive person. I don't know how I existed before; it's like I'm noticing everything for the first time." Suddenly I notice one of the twelve-year-old girls with her eyes riveted upon me.

"It seems that you've touched Josie somehow. She's on the edge of her chair, she's listening so hard." Dede smiles at her. "Do you understand what Barb is saying, honey?"

There is a flash of delight and understanding. "Yes," she murmurs.

What can I say? I look at the kids and then the adults. "Probably I'm about Josie's age right now, just have to learn it all over again."

Vicki speaks, very quietly, "No, Barbara, you're wrong. It is not a question of relearning; you just never had the chance . . . Why, I bet you've never fallen in love."

I looked at her sharply. How do you know, baby? How does anybody know? The talk goes on, half-bright, half-serious; but I'm no longer a part of it. I've torn myself away from the skin of this Game and am alone again. Finally Dede says, "Well, Barbara, we'll continue this soon." He looks at the Sister and the adults with the ten children listening and he says, "I think all of us feel we've learned something." He takes the young Sister's hand and says, "For me, today's Stew is a special treat! As I watch the metamorphosis of Sister Barbara, I see my own self a few years ago and the growth that was once and is still continuing."

The young Sister gets up to leave and stiffens slightly as if she'd like to say, "I only know, Sir, that henceforward, I shall count my days at Synanon like pennies . . . That death can't begin to be worth what you pay for it in life." And the young Sister, me, goes outside to the beach.

# Sister Thomas Wolfe

The young Sister, me, Sister Thomas Wolfe, begins this thought:

Who at twenty-two ended up here at Synanon, in the summer with the sand warm and the sea foamy and fearful. Who is not Roberta-the-addict nor Fran-the-prostitute, but could very well be. Could very well be not Sister Snow-white but Lady Red, whose wedding to the world will not be in a white cake dress.

Who by some inexplicable fate has come to understand that she is not privileged nor lucky. That she knows nothing, that her words fall apart like sand, that her body is cumbersome and thick; that she knows nothing except that her life here, now, and her life there, someday, is and will no longer be dependent upon the caste-mold, the parents, brothers, friends, schools, but upon herself. That Roberta and Fran may never become what she is now, nor she them, yet suddenly, here, standing on the warm sand and the foamy, fearless sea, she realizes that they are better off, for they have loved. My God, do you hear that? She's never loved.

And,

> Siddhartha stood still and for a moment an icy chill stole over him. He shivered inwardly like a small animal, like a bird or a hare, when he realized how alone he was. [H. Hesse *Siddhartha,* p. 43.]

# Pure gold sunburn

One must treat it as a wart. A wart can be picked at, cut off, even burned down, yet it won't disappear. Until quite suddenly it goes of its own accord. My father says ninety percent of all warts are of this ornery type. So I will treat the temptation as a wart. I will wait until the thought of Vance leaves of its own accord.

The day singes my eyelashes. Poor Father Mike. He had spent an entire Sunday at the hot, California beach.

"Just treat me as a post-Fourth of July sparkler," he says weakly as he eases into the back seat of Vicki's car.

We drive to Vicki's house in the Santa Monica hills. We have to park the car below the house and struggle on foot through the summer leaves until we get up to it. Just as I hoped —a house sheltered by trees, very arty, made of glass and wood. Vicki's husband, who plays Games with the Mamas and Papas, is a furniture maker.

In the center of her bamboo living room, is a glass table shaped like an hour glass. There are a multitude of bright straw flowers on it.

"Larry made this, too?"

"Oh, yes." She touches it lightly.

How wonderful to have a creative husband! I look at the huge black and white photographs framed on the walls.

Vicki follows my eyes. "Yes. Those were done during my photographer stage. That's really what I started out as in Synanon."

"You taught photography?"

"Yes, then art. I got so involved in it that Mandy started school at Synanon. Now I'd like to teach something else, but—"

"But Al won't let you?" I smile.

"Right. Hey, listen, you two, make yourselves at home and I'll get dinner ready."

Mike sits gingerly on the sofa. He tries to lean back, holding his suntan lotion as if it were Linus' blanket, "You'd think I'd wise up," he mutters.

"I've done it, too. If it hurts enough this time you'll learn." I relax in a chair, admiring the polished wood floors, all light and trees inside and out, flowers everywhere, fragments of one's own work and life. "Oh, Vicki, your house is great! The kind of place I'd love."

"Yeah, Vicki, it's all Bucky Fuller—you've created a very livable environment here," Mike says limply.

"There you go, Mike. Buckminister Fuller—Don't you ever stop teaching?" I say, meaning it as a compliment because he's such a fine teacher.

" 'S funny," Mike says, "but my discipline is drama and English, and I thought Al was nuts suggesting Bucky Fuller, but I'm really enjoying it."

"So are the kids," Vicki adds as she brings us some quinine water.

"What I'd do for a nice scotch," Mike looks distastefully at his drink.

"I could get you some," Vicki rises.

"Nope. As long as I'm in Synanon, I'll keep the rules." He sips his drink, and Vicki leaves to fix the dinner. "But, Mike," I protest, "I thought you were going to stay here."

"Are you kidding? Who told you that?" He puts his drink down.

"I don't know. I just heard it around."

"Rumors. Nope, Six weeks, all right, but no more. This place has more rules than the Church!" His gentle face reddens.

"You're not kidding," I laugh. "And what gets me, Mike, is that they're continually knocking religious life for having too many regulations!"

"They're kinda behind the times!"

"*Slightly*. Why, I saw a man yesterday carrying a telephone around."

"Why?"

"It seems he'd made a long distance telephone call without permission, so they made him carry a phone around all day."

Mike slaps his knee. "Oh!" he grimaces with pain and laughter. "Sounds like a Novitiate practice to me."

"Well, listen to this one . . . This young guy had to go to L.A. County Hospital for some reason, and while he was there he smoked pot. So do you know what they did to him when he got back?"

"Let's see." Mike strokes his face thoughtfully. "I bet he had to wear a pot around his neck all day."

"And to think that sort of crap was part of our training!"

"Yeah, this place is too constricting—the School, the Club itself, the Games, a person's just got to be free." He tries to relax, but his sunburn is killing him.

"You're right, Mike, and yet—I thought that same way once, but I've seen Synanon from the inside out, since my Trip. It really works."

"Oh, you don't have to tell me that. I've seen how it's changed my brother, Ted, but I couldn't stay."

"Why not?"

"I want to be a priest."

"I won't quibble with that, Mike. But—I don't know. Synanon just does it so much better." And I tell him the incident about the girl who smothered her baby.

"And all those people forgave her?" He looks at me steadily.

"Yes, it was really the only answer. Sure, she has to make her peace with God—but that can't be done in isolation. We can't forgive ourselves, our stupidity, until we're sure that others do."

"A sort of group absolution, then?"

"Yes, led by your brother."

"Hmm. My brother." And I know he must be thinking about Ted, so much stronger than himself. And I suddenly want to tell Mike that all that drugs did to Ted was—well, they made him a man. Or Synanon has. And Father Mike? He seems so soft to me, like—suntan lotion.

"Barb, I didn't know him very well. We lived two different lives. I've been in the seminary since I was thirteen. And he's been on the streets."

"Is that why so many priests are getting married?" I ask. "Because they've been out of it so long?"

"No, I don't think so."

"Maybe they're just not afraid anymore. They're not like laymen, full of pious superstitions; they've seen authority up close. They've been inside the Holy House; they know it's pretty rotten."

"Then let it be rotten. It doesn't destroy my faith. Christ isn't rotten."

"Yes, I know," I answer quietly. "Life is full of holes, but Christ is pure gold inside."

I look at him. "Will you ever leave?" I ask.

"To get married, you mean?"

I nod.

"No—I'm a quiet man, my needs are few," he pulls the room together with his hands. "I like beautiful places, a good movie, the Mass, the teenagers I work with back in Poughkeepsie. If I left, I'd go on doing what I'm doing now—" he smiles at me.

"Synanon?"

"No. Synanon's not ready for people like me."

The meal we eat is mixed with gall and yogurt. Vicki serves us fried chicken and spiced tea flavored with brown sugar. But all I'm thinking during that whole dinner is that chastity is a sunburn: sometimes it means being drenched with pain.

# Chocolate Vance

"Yeah," I say. "I know how it is. A funeral feeling coming on; I mean *grave*." I wave goodbye to Roberta as I go out of the apartment.

Going to chuck this weary, worri*some* world and find him. Vance. He said Wednesday night was his Game night. So down to the Club—I know a lot of people now. It's about an hour before the Games, so I sit in a booth with a bunch of women from my Trip.

"You're going to tell your mother about your Trip?" I ask Judy.

"Oh, I did. Sunday night, as soon as I got home . . . I came in the back door and she met me. We sat on the floor and talked until 2 A.M." She laughs. "It was great."

"Oh," I answer.

Joan leans towards me. "You *should* tell her, you know, Barb."

"Yeah," I answer and get up quickly. Gregory. Is that weak-kneed Gregory? I can't really tell. He's wearing a mod turtle neck and a plaid jacket. Gregory? But he does have a bald head.

"Barbara!" He takes my hand. "I can't seem to find my tribe."

"Are you in the Omegas?" That's Vance's tribe.

"Yes . . . Yes, I am! *Sir!*" he calls to a resident near us. "Oh, a barbecue. At the Clump?" He looks at me. "How do I get there?"

Vance . . . "Oh, I'm going that way; I'll direct you."

We go outside to the parking lot and he helps me into his silver XKE. Gregory? I smile to myself. How different he seemed in a brown robe.

Getting into a sports car is a metaphor for a low mood. One is sure others can see to one's depths. Does my slip show? One can long for a habit for many reasons—it covers a multitude of fleshy sins.

We go over to the pool area at the Clump where the fifty

or so members of Gregory's tribe are gathered. They are watching various members gallantly get their heads shaved.

A bald head. Vance!

With a few eyes upon me, I run over toward him.

"Barbara!" I notice how beautiful his eyes are against tanned skin. He gives me a hug and introduces me around.

Then he sits down on his haunches and laughingly takes the arm of the guy next to him, "So I tell her, baby—" and all the men laugh. Across the pool I watched two men get their heads shaved.

"Well. Aah, goodbye, Vance," I interrupt him.

He untangles his long body and stands. "Yeah. I'll see you around, Barb. Glad everything's going so swell for you." He waves me off.

Then, walking home. God. A person should be able to decide when she will fall in love. It's all too droopy for me, a weight sitting on my mind and heart. This desire for candy. It's all right. One piece of semi-sweet chocolate and I'll be fine.

# Mary made for birthdays

I walk down toward the beach. It is late afternoon, The playground equipment on Muscle Beach is clanging in the summer wind. Ruth Stein calls them the ghost children playing on the rings. I take my glasses off.

For me, when I have my glasses on, everything is delineated, like clear, logical thought. Glasses off, everything is fuzz, like pure emotion. Or loneliness. No one can touch me because I can't see them.

It is a day of loneliness: the gull tells me by his whispered wings and the rocks gouge it into my feet. Is this what I'm going to do the rest of my life? Sublimate? Instead of a man, candy? Instead of children, teaching? Instead of the erotic, poetry? Instead of life, the convent? My neck burns as I say these words, for I'm still thinking of Vance.

And this is what gets me. I'm the one staying in the convent, yet I'm the one fighting so hard this summer about chastity. And Mary? She's the one's who's leaving, yet she's taken what seems to me the unrealistic position of trying to remain a virgin in the world while not having the support of a community. She's thinking about staying at Synanon as a *celibate*. When she told me, I laughed in her face, "You're nuts. Synanon is Old Testament: fecundity, my deah," imitating an old Scripture scholar we once had.

She laughed, "I just don't feel such a need for sex, Barbara."

I stared at her.

"Well," she continued, "Ah—not the way you do. Barb—" she ended very quietly, "sometimes I think, well, in comparison to you, that I'm—frigid."

I adjusted my glasses on my nose. "God, Mary, don't let Synanon screw you up! I think it's great that you want to remain a virgin—I'm just saying I don't think you can do it without a celibate community to help you." She looked at me with her ocean-eyes, and I remember the men who have liked her here, especially Mannie and John, and I know she couldn't bear the spring without a man. I see her unlocking her apartment door at night and no one there except echoes. She wouldn't last.

I've got to talk to her today. The old, creaky Synanon schoolhouse tells me in its own way that loneliness is naked, gouged, whispered. And Mary—there's got to be a special heaven for her. She was made for birthdays: a yellow birthday cake for God with *enjoy! enjoy!* written on it in a chain of daisies; and all of us having place cards, paper hats on our heads, balloons floating everywhere and gifts for free.

Now I want to be reassured that such a birthday place exists. I sit down on one of the beach swings and force myself up high—There she is, walking around a small patch of grass near the Pier.

I watch her go around the circle a long time, until I can watch no longer; by the bend of her head, I know. All knuckles and knees and er-ah, she's my friend. I run to her across the sand, and we walk for a long while, arms thrown around shoulders. My arm feels what she can't say, and I'm thinking back to the time in the convent when we were invited up to the snow for a weekend. At that stage of the Novitiate, we weren't allowed to wear anything in public except our habits. Everyone else stayed comfortable inside the warm cabin, but Sister Mary and I. We each put on five coats, and lumbering like two huge black bears, prayed for hours in the snow. I remember the snowflakes heavy on her eyelashes; and wondering what it was like to see the world through such eyes.

Mary used to be programmed to certain key words. Out on the beach, walking in the coming twilight, feeling the heavings of her shoulders, I could have said: children! flying kites! prayer! the Father! and once she would have fallen apart like a flower. But that was *no good* now.

I walk in her steps; when she slows down to kick seaweed, so do I, and my arms feel the nerves of her body tighten. She says, "It's good to be your sister."

And then she tells me how they've put John Nicholas on a ban from all women. It seems instead of going to work a few days ago, he borrowed the car from Medical and took Mary out to dinner with his mother and then down to the beach.

Then she stops walking and says, "Barb—I think he loves me." I don't know what to answer except that "John loves anybody who'll give him an ear. But dingbat that he is, the last one who gave him an ear got preg—"

"Shut up." She glares at me. She's holding the old torn, paperback Bible in her hand. "You sound just like Synanon! I know John is pitiable but he tries. I explained to him about my belief in chastity and—"

"Yes—" I say, kicking the cold sand.

"He understands, Barb—I mean, perhaps, he'll just accept it because he believes in me, and that's why this ban is stupid!"

"He knows the rules, Mary. Stay away from him. He got what he deserved."

Her mouth drops. "My God, Barbara." She begins to cry. "You're beginning to sound like you were born here!"

I cover my face. Synanon is bulging out of my head! I wish I were the three monkeys holding my eyes, ears, and mouth. Keep out Synanon, let me keep my friend, my life.

Yet neither whispered wings, nor rock's gouge, nor naked house can keep them away. Love would not permit God to shut his door.

# *The mockingbird of the body*

Roberta smiles at my question. I can see the curve of her breast through her nightgown. She turns on her side and says, "What does it for a woman? Is it that ol' mockingbird singin' somewhere in your mind? You dance, sit at bars, sip scotch, and wait. Like life, for a woman, is just waitin'. Oh, once it comes it's goin', but there's still waitin' in it, too.

"Sometimes when I'm walkin' to the library by myself, I think about it. Is it the buyin' all the time? The hollow feelin' in the gut, tryin' to cover it up with a visit to Newberry's or whatever to buy"—she touches the horoscope booklet on the bedside table, "even this? To get it out of you—givin' it away, if you must.

"Is it that ol' mockingbird in your mind that you run from? Or the buyin'? So, good God, you make yourself nice. You watch an' wait an' listen an' need because—well, I'll tell you, Barbara. Nuns don't have a hold on longin' . . . Even a man's not goin' t' stop that ol' mockingbird, Goddamn, not ever. That ol' bird will keep singin' in the corner of your body until you die an' nothin'll stop him until you die. An' you know what, Barbara?"

I raise my eyes, "What?"

"I think that even when you die he'll still be singin' cuz he's life, girl, life. Life don't ever stop cryin' in you, askin' for more than you give it. Life keeps beggin' for more until you die, pushin' out your best to it, pushin' out your youth to it in great squirts of children an' lovin', howsomever you give it."

She stops. Smiles at me. "But what you goin' to do now, girl? Now that you've seen the light? What you gonna do?"

"See Al Bauman," I answer.

# A thousand pairs of nylons

"But what makes you think that Synanon will accept you, my dear?" Al lights another cigarette.

"Pardon me?" I stammer.

He lifts his ice-blue eyes from the ash tray. "You heard me, asshole. What makes you think we want you?"

I stare at Al.

"You see, Barbara, you may be a passable teacher but we don't have such a great demand for teachers—do we, Ruth?"

She glances up from her writing and comments, "We had another application today."

Al takes a drag off his cigarette. "The point is, you'd be a great bother to us. All that re-education—do you think you could stand it?"

I'm not feeling too well. "What do you mean?"

"Well, for instance, you've had quite a bit of freedom as a summer resident. We put you in as a teacher immediately, instead of making you work your way up—"

Yeah, work my way up to ten hours of teaching a day and two bucks a week . . . I try to smile, "I don't need to work up. After all, I know my responsibilities."

"Bullshit, Barbara."

Shall I answer, "Nice alliteration, Al"? The difference between Dede Harvey and Al Bauman is the difference between sugar and granite. I stare at him.

Al stares back. He puts his hand on his huge forehead, made even higher by his bald head. "Do you think I came into Synanon and was made schoolmaster immediately? I worked at construction and then began in the School—and don't think you'd continue to live at the Kansas apartments—they are a luxury you don't deserve. You'd start out in the dorms like everyone else."

The dorms? Me trying to read a book while being engulfed by one thousand pairs of nylons and hair curlers, the noise of radios and talk. I stick my chin out. "I believe in Synanon, Al.

I've seen it work—but I wasn't planning to stay on after the summer, anyway."

"Why not?" He lights another cigarette. I don't believe I've ever seen Al without a cancerstick in hand.

"I have my responsibilities to my life as a nun. I told them I would stay another year. I don't want to break that."

He brushes the ashes off the table. "You won't come back after a year."

My anger strikes at him, "How do you know?"

"I know—"

"What?" I ask.

"Al," Ruth interrupts, "may I tell Barbara something?"

He smiles for the first time, "Yes."

Ruth touches her short red hair. "Anyone who can dance like you, Barbara, *must stay* . . . You should have seen her, Al! I never noticed before what a marvelous rhythm you have!"

Too delighted to make humility graceful, I mutter, "I wasn't a good dancer before; I mean I couldn't do my old thing until the Trip. Until I began to feel twenty-two again."

Al cocks his head. "Nice feeling?"

"Yes, very nice."

"Stay with us, Barb." His face changes.

I get up to leave. What can I say? If I stay at Synanon, I'll be copping out on my Sisters. I've learned so much; they'll only listen if I return and take up their life-style again.

I should go back to my work at the School but instead I go to a root beer stand near the Club.

I haven't changed much. I still hate to work, and watch the clock like a doctor watches a heartbeat. I'm hungry all the time. All I really have to do is open my ample mouth, and I suck up the world. I should talk to Fran before this feeling goes. Mother. It's time I went home.

# Cucumbers in sour cream

I'm sitting in my mother's dining room eating cucumbers in sour cream. In front of me there are white gardenias floating in a blue bowl. My mother and father are here. The dog is playing with our cat, Arthur, in the kitchen. I look up from my cucumbers and realize that mother is another collector, like Dan Marsh: curios, vases, pictures from a lifetime of voyages, are everywhere.

Once I had a dream that I lost my family. I frantically search the battered world for them but to no avail. Then one day, as I'm standing in a cafeteria line, there's a man eating cucumbers in sour cream—it's my father. Further on, there's a young man eating cucumbers in sour cream and it's my brother. So here I am, eating cucumbers in sour cream and my Mom and Dad are at both ends of the table, and Anna, my Mom's good friend, is speaking to me.

"Trip? L.S.D.? At Synanon?"

"No, no. Not acid. Like it's getting together in a very communal relationship with about fourteen people in a space of forty-eight hours—which is really six days when you . . ." So I run them the story. I leave out some parts. Can't tell them about Fran and the picture on the blackboard. Nor about Sean and the hand touch. But I tell them most of it, except about Joan. I've come home to tell my Mom about Joan, but I can't.

The rugs are old and worn beneath my feet. I remember when they were fluffy and I could feel the new carpet tacks as I walked upstairs.

The old square-foot T.V. is gone. Affluence has brought us a color one, a stereo, a tape recorder. Even Michael, our cocker, has been replaced by Michael II, our terrier; soon it will be autumn.

Daddy gets up to pour the coffee and then sits across from me at the dining room table. Anna is at the far end and Mother is very near to me. I turn slightly so that I'm facing her.

"Mom?" I begin.

"Yes?" She sips her coffee.

"Something very peculiar happened on the Trip. Like it was between two other people and it sorta caromed onto me . . ." I'm searching her face; the freckles have almost left her. They've stretched out as if they, too, are tired.

"*What* was between two people?" she asks.

So I run her the story about Joan and Fran—about her and me. *How many times will I forgive my mother? my daughter? Seventy times seven?* I watched her face very closely. *Harden not your heart as you did in Santa Monica.*

For a moment, my Mom is fragile in my eyes. For a moment, she is standing outdoors with the wind brushing her hair across her face. She is twenty-two and going around the world for the first time.

Anna asks my Dad if he wants more coffee. She leaves the table while he begins to clear the dishes.

But they don't feel it like us, do they, Mom? Her face trembles like when she gives me a present; anxious to see if I'll like it.

It's fine, Mom. It's the best moment you've ever given me because I know you understand. Hey! Old lady, don't cry. God—I'm choking on cold cucumbers.

# Rings

"They've what, Mary?" I lean over her.

"They've kicked John out! Can't you hear me?" She blows her nose, and looks up at me, "He was on that ban from all women, remember?"

I laugh. "Yeah . . ."

"Then today he went over to see his wife and their child. He was playing with his little boy when they came to get him."

"Why did they come?"

She jerks her head up, "Because he was on a ban and wasn't supposed to see his wife. And they told him that they were sick of babysitting him and that he'd been at Synanon for two and a half years and hadn't grown a bit. So they took him to the end of the world and dropped him off. Oh, Barbara, what will happen to him?"

There's nothing to tell her. I'm just thinking about that little wisp of a man, John Nichol, standing on a dark street in L.A. called "the end of the world" with a dollar in his pocket.

"I'll never understand Synanon's thinking, Barbara."

I look at her. There was a dream I had of stepping down from a very high place.

The men who greeted us were dressed identically in suits with Nehru collars. They each had a flashing ring on their wedding band fingers.

I remember the dirt, the tracks, and their unflinching faces. I smiled and saluted; a young man with a clown face and baggy pants saluted me back.

They took us down a flat street to a freshly built house. The front steps still had dirt upon them. A bulldozer was parked a few paces off. Up the whole block there were one-story houses, all identical. Peeling white paint with pink geraniums. A small Negro boy was looking out. And I said to myself, it doesn't change; they do no better here than elsewhere.

The living room was furnished in the dead, early-'50's style. There were floor lamps and a yellowish carpet. In what room were we when the young man with the clown face turned to his officer and said he loved me? "She reminds me—it's like being back in college, again."

Standing near a bookcase, unable to control my curiosity, I read everything. Among the little announcement cards I found one that said:

INTERCOURSE 10th and 20th
OF THE MONTH *ONLY*

I thought, my God, how tragic.

We were each given a ring. My ring meant that I was only a temporary guest, although it could be exchanged for a lifetime ring at any time.

I heard them talking. The clown-faced young man wanted me and was going to ask to court me. The officer answered, "Only if she exchanges her ring." The artificiality of the place didn't matter any more because I loved the clown-faced man madly. He became a groove in my mind and I was constantly returning to him, constantly making my thoughts spin under his cool needle.

Yet I did not want to exchange my ring.

One night the clown-faced man came to see me. We had a long talk and I tried to explain why I had to keep my temporary ring. He listened very quietly. Then I got up to arrange the white gardenias.

I stood in the dark kitchen and the white petals gleamed in my hands. My head went back and forth with the gardenias' scent. Then I felt him coming near me in the dark. My ring sparkled, the flowers became heavy in my hands.

Finally, it was the 10th of the month. My clown-faced man was performing in an endless play. He was the hero, and the man in the gold Roman-collared turtle neck, who lay all day in the huge bed listening to baroque records, was the enemy. Scattered through the audience were men and boys that I had loved, but I wanted the play to end. I wanted my clown-faced man.

"You fool, Barbara. Why are you exchanging your ring?" a boy with a big nose asked me.

"I don't know . . . I want him. It doesn't matter." And I thought I smelled gardenias.

"You're not afraid?" a red haired man asked quietly.

"I'm scared to death. A woman can lose everything by doing something like this."

I think of John. A man can lose everything, too. Yet I knew, even in my dream, that one must take the risk.

I don't tell Mary my dream. I have no public answer for her.

# *Where all women go sometime*

To be a woman is to walk past the hard stares of men in the tight alley of life. You may reject their entrance (waiting for the one, the One), yes, but all the time you're thinking of the joy latent in your body. Like a snake, you desire to molt your skin so that the joy within you can burst free—but the man is the snake. And the woman? God, a mama cow, a sheep, a she-cat—anything with a fat belly and swinging tits.

So you say to life, in choir-nun fashion: *I accept your right to take me, Sir. I accept your ability to slice a hole in the night and take me in a sea where all women must have gone, sometime—half crying, laughing, tears mixed with sweat, tangled in you, life: glad, soft, working God working, to be open.*

*I accept your right, Sir, to get inside me. And this only do I warn you: do not put yourself in so vulnerable a place of responsibility (pink and white mushrooms, touch and see, they stiffen) unless you are willing to be revealed.*

*I accept you, Sir. Finally. Certainly, not as I accepted God. He came easily into my soul compared to you (I understood innocence). You came hard. You came train-lightning: we shuddered (I did not understand).*

Must it, does it, always (the young girl begs), does it always hurt like this? She says it with her eyes. She is looking toward Dede and Al in the children's Stew.

Al lights a cigarette. "Yes—it's very painful for most women. But the great delight is that these women do exist."

"Yes—women who aren't albatrosses," Dede comments.

"What do you mean, albatross?" I ask.

Al smiles. "College girl hasn't read Coleridge?" Not even polite. No wonder he has such rotten teeth, they've been bitten off by his barbs.

I don't smile. "The bird that follows him everywhere?"

"Correct—at Synanon, we mean by albatross, the woman who hangs around a man's neck and won't let him be free, who continually pulls him lower and lower. The ambitious woman, the nagger. One of the ways a woman gets that way is overriding her husband's work (he looks over at Dede). I want Joan relieved of some of her jobs. She is doing well but—" He flicks his cigarette.

Al's wife, Nina, leans forward. "What do you mean, Al. Shouldn't a woman be involved with her husband's work?"

Al jerks his head. "Now did I say that? There you go again, Nina, making an overstatement about something quite open."

I don't know how Nina maintains her patience. She answers quietly, "How do you mean?"

"I didn't say a wife shouldn't be interested. I merely said that a woman needs time to *be* a woman." He looks over at Dede again. "A man needs a cove. He needs a woman who can make a place of warmth for him." Al rubs his forehead. "You know how it is—talking, running this way and that, noise, chatter, irritations—to come home to a place like that?"

Dede smiles slightly. "Yeah—"

"With more noise, chatter, bang-bang, because she, too, runs, backs up, shoves, good God!" He leans back. "Our best moments—Nina's and mine, have been when I come home and she's there and it is peace—flowers."

Dede shifts his pants. "Yeah."

"A man needs a clean, well-lighted place to come home to . . . the woman has to have *some* time to create that atmosphere —that environment. She has to be what her form tends toward —a cove."

It is time for me to go back to my workshop. I smile quietly at that smartass, Al. The good, proud, crystal man.

I go to my window and watch the Santa Monica sea. And God, who was also man, got used to walking waters. *Carry me, Sir, to a sea where all women must go sometime.*

# Snow castles

When I get home from the School, I begin to read a short story by Joyce Carol Oates called "The Census Taker."

A young census taker comes to a backwood house and waits in the kitchen until the man of the house returns. He talks quietly to the wife, until the young daughter and son come in. He mentions how tired he is.

> "Why don't you just fall asleep?" the girl said.
>
> The mother turned sharply. "You, Rose ANN!" she said.
>
> "But why don't he? It's what I mean to do. I ain't goin' to keep on, no walled-in world, no numbers writ down in a book to stand for me," the girl said spitefully, passionately. "I ain't goin' through the old ways—not comin' from a child to a woman, havin' children to keep on with the old ways, sufferin' them, sufferin' all agony to squeeze them out in no walled-in world! An' sick all your life, an' poor, an' got to get up in the mornin' to ice on the window. I ain't goin' through the old ways! . . . I ain't! I'm goin' asleep. No cancer for me, I can feel it eating in my body already . . . We watched an' listened to our grandma die that way, jumpin' around on the bed. How I mean to do, I mean to have a man, once to know THAT, an' go on out to the snow an' sleep. Them people of this world, why, go through the old ways like a horse pullin' a plow, goin' through the ruts. I ain't goin' to do that."

After reading this, I try to fall asleep. But all I do is think.

Them people of this world don' know how it is with us virgins. Them people think it's jest fine to be taffeta, snow, sheets. Them people don' know, don' got no idea, what*so*ever, how it is to be a question mark. You jest ain't nothin' til you give yerself away, 'til someone gets inside you, and your freedom's all gone, all given to him, throbbing inside you.

And sure, Ma, sure it's easy to be real proud of a virgin daughter, your agnostic plastic holy mary sittin' on your bureau top in framed pictures of high school graduation and nun life, etc. But yer daughter, see, she jest don't see all that worth, no mam, she don'.

Them people of this world freeze life in their ice boxes, see, or, in their pitcher frames, or in their auto-*ma*-tic televisions with the pyramid eye like the one on a dollar bill but that ain't life, no sure. Life ain't anything but one man and one woman seekin' each other out through all the route 66's of their times.

Life ain't nothin' but their lovin' and the stuff that goes on there in the snow with the rain drippin' hail on them and turnin' the snow to mush and meltin' the snow and them lyin' there and lovin' and to hell with all them people of this world and their ruts!

The hell with it all, an jes' you and me and the snow buildin' castles around us, and the sleep, with the grass building secretly, and high, beneath our soul . . .

# *Waiting for a prince*

"God, Mary! There must be some pure place in the world! There must be some people bent on being pure! Yes, they're weak, but they try," I jut my jaw out.

"I'm not saying that, Barb. I'm saying that—"

"But you *are*. Don't you see what they're doing to us? You know kicking John—poor, weak, pitiable John—out was cruel. To punish him, yes, but to kick him out was shit, Mary. Shit. And just because you talk to Terry Hurst, the President's wife, doesn't make it all right, does it? What's going to happen to him, don't you think about *that*?"

She glares at me. "I do—all the time."

I look at her for a moment. "So what's happening to us? What are we becoming in just a few months in this pressure cooker? I almost went crazy watching you and Mannie last Saturday night."

"What in the hell are you talking about?" she juts *her* jaw out.

"I don't know how to say it . . . I mean those people were there talking to me and I was going crazy as I watched you and Mannie . . ." I finger the ash tray ". . . because, well, I had this little shiver in me that something *bad* was going to happen and hell, Mary, I didn't know what to do."

She relaxes on the sofa. "Well, why didn't you come up? Why didn't you call me away and say something?"

"Like I couldn't, I tell you, I had to entertain those people, and Ray was there. So I'm sitting there talking about drug addiction and I'm watching you and Mannie out of the corner of my eye . . . I can barely see you because you're lost behind the high rails of the lounge sofas—"

She stiffens. "Oh, all right, Barbara. All right. We, we did leave."

I gulp, "You did?"

"People . . . kept staring."

I wipe my mouth. "I—I, I'm sorry, Mary. I just felt this shiver and I didn't, I mean, didn't mean to pry."

"*Shut up,* Barbara! Let me . . . Let me tell you," she looks down at her bony hands. "He—he took me upstairs to his room in the Club."

And I'm thinking to myself that if that Puerto Rican dingbat dared do anything, if he dared hurt her, I'll—

"He kissed me, Barb," her long lashes brush against her tan face. "I—I wanted him, but I couldn't. I just froze—it wasn't right. I don't care what *they* say, it wasn't right!"

I touch her. "Mary, *see?* What has become . . . ?" I let my hands fall. "Even Synanon knows . . . Sometimes I think they'd like us to stay as we are. You know, something funny happened with Ray and me at the Saturday night party."

She wipes her eyes again. "Yes?"

"Well, my friends, Margie and Kristin were talking with Danny. And Ray asked me to dance a slow one. So we're dancing, see. He's got on his baggy overalls and he looks like such a clown. And we're dancing about a foot apart." I make a gesture with my hands, "and George comes up."

"Which George?" she asks.

I laugh. "George-the-cook. The black guy from the School."

"Oh." She lights a cigarette.

"And he motions that he wants to talk to Ray. Finally, Ray comes back. Do you know what George had to say to him?"

"Something about you and Ray? What?" She leans toward me.

"Yes. He said, 'Remember, kid, her position here. Synanon doesn't want her to become the fucking-nun.' "

Mary laughs, "Too much!"

"But really, it's a pretty great thing. They do care about us."

"Yes," she smiles. She looks up at me with the end part of her unrolling thoughts, "Whatever it's done to us . . . I know that some good things have occurred."

I'm dejected. "Like what?"

"Our friendship has grown. We've . . . shared our needs together." She laughs a little to herself. "Sometimes, I feel I'm waiting for my prince to come."

I turn from the window. "God, yes! We're always waiting for a prince to come. I remember once, after a real happy dinner with the community, Sister David Marie left us to go to her duties. We were laughing so hard that we forgot to help her—

having such a good time and all. There she was, out there alone in the kitchen, washing *our* dishes. And a Superior!"

"Yes!"

"So Sister Jacquelyn and I finally realize it and zoom to the kitchen. There she is alone. Her arms deep in suds and one, bare light swinging above her. Jacquelyn laughs and sings, "Someday your prince will come." And I laugh outright, Cinderella! But it's always waiting for a prince to come."

She lays her hand on my arm. "And the Kingdom."

"You know," I muse aloud. "I was free in the convent. How could I stay in a place like Synanon? Where casual sex is almost the rule, kids are separated from their parents and cruelty"—I tighten my first—"is commended? I love some of their ideas—like self-reliance being central—and I told you about Al's discussion in the Stew about womanhood. But God, Mary," I hold my ears, "sex is bulging out my head! The one thing I'd really like to do is walk through the trees by our convent."

"What trees? I always remember Palos Verdes as bare."

"Bare? Why, there's a cluster of high trees on the right side of the playground. I used to go there often after Robert Kennedy's death. Just to walk and pray."

"But you can't do that *all* the time?" She sits down in a chair hard.

"Who said that? But I do miss the nuns and the old place—even the way it sprawls all over the grounds. Really, I suppose it was nice at first, but they kept building additions. At first, it was shaped like a capital I, then an L, then an E, and when I see it next, it'll probably be an O."

"Why an O?"

" 'O Barbara, what have you become?' the house will say to me. And I'll answer, 'O house, I have become.' O Mary, what shall I do?"

"What do you mean?" She's at my side.

"I don't know . . . I have to get away from this place. Synanon's pressing on my head."

"Where will you go?" she asks.

"I'll go to our convent in the Valley."

# *Thank god, she's a virgin again*

Okay, God, this is it. I've got responsibilities, man. Remember me? Sad nun at Synanon.

Once I made a retreat at Valyermo, a Benedictine monastery. A young Benedictine novice, Brother Gregory, I believe, spoke eloquently about God and prayer. But it's hard to trust novices much: remember, I was one once. I know what it's like to be God's balloon at nineteen. But Brother Gregory was almost believable; rich, expressive lips, and a rather heavy nose; looked as if he approached life luxuriously, by smelling it.

He said, "The Benedictine way of prayer is very simple. It is to eat Scripture—to digest it in moments of great longing. To speak to God without words, to become faceless before him."

"Faceless?" I repeated.

"Yes—to no longer own anything . . . We Benedictines have a very severe form of poverty; we own nothing, not even our own bodies."

And then I felt sorry for him. Not for allowing himself to be given to God and his fellowman to be eaten like Scripture. For a free man, this is truly a great vocation. To become faceless before God, yes, our face is such a small thing, meant to be given away. God must get more tired than we do of genuflections, our long introductions, our Thees and Thous. It's good to be before Him without roles. But to lose one's body is to lose one's soul. Is there a greater loss at nineteen?

Of course, I didn't say any of this to the novice. But I thought to myself that one's spirit is in the seams of one's body. To be naked before God, yes. To face each other and God with the small knob of your being is good, too. But, do I believe in the possibility of giving myself away? Can the central part of that gift be the loss of my dance?

I'm feeling rather ambiguous arriving at the good old convent. It's so hot outside I almost freeze my buns off (*Barbara! cut the Synanonese*) stepping into the stillness of its newly air-conditioned interior. It's good to be sucked into the nun's life there. After dinner, they keep pumping me about Synanon.

"Well, if you're asking, if you really want to know how I feel . . . a pause—we nuns don't know a damn thing about sex. I mean, we pat it on the head, saying (because we're liberal now) that sex is God's gift and all that jazz, but we don't ever really consider its centrality or its power." Then I stop in mid-air, like it's a new type of rosary lecture.

Sister Victoire adjusts her pillow on the community room rug. "How do you mean?"

"D'ya know what one dingbat asked me at Synanon a little while back?" I let the question interest them. "He says, 'You mean to tell me those nuns don't want a good fuck?' And I answered him, honestly (because I really think it's true), 'No. We don't. A woman can find a certain ecstasy with God—I mean, if she really prays, gut-praying, I guess you'd call it—then He's enough.' I mean, if you think about it (and I don't think we do, enough), God is the completely sexual." The first indication that maybe I'm being too frank is when Sister Jeanne Marie kind of giggles. I watch her thick lips quiver until Sister Victoire scowls at her.

"You've got a real point there, Sister Barbara,"—I smile, hearing myself being called Sister again—"it's true . . ." She flicks her blond hair to the side and looks at Sisters Jeanne Marie, Brigid, and Roberta, "do we ever discuss sex?"

Sister Brigid wipes her nunny-glasses. "No. Or, rarely.'

"Here we're supposed to be teaching teenage girls about *life,* and we never—" I make a gesture of hopelessness with my hands. "Take the Birth Control encyclical. The day it was issued, Father Mike and I went into the kid's Stew to discuss it."

Roberta gives me her apple-smile. "You forget we don't share your new lingo, Barb."

"A Stew's like an extended game, a type of sensitivity session or encounter group, where most of the educational process of Synanon goes on . . . Well, imagine yourself in a large circle with about forty kids. Dede Harvey's there, too (he's an ex-minister and new headmaster of the School), besides Dorothy Salant, Father Mike, and me. The kids are universally in agreement that Pope Paul is so far from life as we grovelings live it that they want to tell him how it is.

"Kathy Hurst says, 'Pope Paul is afraid to drop his image—to take off his jacket.'

"And Dede says, 'What you Catholics want is to put God on the rocks. To make it practically impossible to believe and live out that belief in day-to-day existence. I know how it is, I once belonged to a Church which said: *Our job is to save you, whether you like it or not.*' Then Dede stares at Father Mike and me. 'Face it, you two,' he says. 'If Jesus came into Synanon, he would say—*this is the place.*'

"And perhaps he's right, I don't know. But I do know that Mike and I would have liked to send the tapes of that Stew to the Holy Father. We couldn't argue with those kids—*they knew.*"

Sister Brigid pulls her skirt further over her knees and smiles. "You mean to tell me you think pre-teen children know more than the Pope?"

"I just think we're being fake. We accept the encyclical only because we aren't faced with the responsibility."

Sister Victoire covers her mouth with her hand and laughs. "No, Barbara, you're incorrect. We accept the encyclical only because we already *are* practicing birth control—the natural way."

I look at her hard. "Natural way? That's your opinion—not that of most people."

She continues slowly, "But don't you think the Church has, perhaps, not only the right, but the necessity—to teach a reverence for life?"

"God, yes, Victoire. One is reminded of that all the time at Synanon, like when waiting for a jitney and a girl slaps her head and cries, 'I've forgotten to take my birth control pills!' Or, the ending of a short story in *Harper's* about a guy who gets an abortion for his girl friend, and when it's all over he says, 'Thank God, she's a virgin again.' But at the same time, we haven't even begun to search for life. Here we usually live with ten or so women and we barely understand what our monthly cycle means in terms of a community of hyper-women."

Someone: "Yes, this loose-confederation-of-available-virgins."

Laughter. "*Please* don't say that too loud around Synanon." The nun's faces.

Somehow, I feel together here. We're not too far apart . . . I'm glad to be home.

# Choosing winter to be born in

"You sound like someone who's about to leave."

I look at Sister Brigid's soft, Italian face.

"Huh?" I sit down in a low chair by her desk.

"I can tell you're unsettled, Barbara. Perhaps you've never been settled. How long have you been a Catholic now?"

"Six years. Good ones. Four years a nun." I try to smile at her. Cold cucumbers again. Sidewise in my throat.

"Just tell me this . . ." She touches my forehead lightly—like I'm a sick child. "Haven't all your years here taught you *anything?* Some greater commitment or responsibility?"

This is the question that burns my soul as I go into the Chapel. It is the first time I've really been alone since the Trip: talk, talk, talk; that's Synanon. Verbal therapy. Talk doesn't give you a hold on faith, does it God? Prophets weren't much for talk. What does St. Paul say? To be put in the hands of the living God is to be touched by a devouring fire.

*O my God.* Shall I borrow a car and go back to Palos Verdes? Shall I crawl before my Superior, Sister David Marie, and pour out my bile? Why? Why do I feel guilty? If I've loved, it was only the strike of one paper match. *My love for you is a paschal candle.*

*And do you, Sister, take this God, this fire, to be your love? Through sickness and joy, until death do unite you?*

Yes. Yes. I do.

*And you, Barbara, do you freely cleave to a mystery as your life?*

Yes.

*A mystery? Never to hold Him to words to explain it?*

Yes. For Christ is the word.

*(But not held by it.) And you, Barbara, will you forgive those who hurt you by not waiting to understand?*

Yes.

*How long is Yes, Barbara?*

Stop burning my soul with questions! I've been happy being a Sister. Any person who freely chooses a life-style is going to have regrets. Particularly, if she's got a well-developed ego like mine. Her dreams will reveal the hundred persons she could have been, all beautiful, always running and finding or making love. If she watches Sophia Loren on T.V., her sleep will make her Sophia Austin. Ten men will be ravaging the world, searching for her.

If she glances at one handsome face, or feels one small question mark, her dreams will remind her: this is so good, so close, why not? *Why not?* And because she is becoming a woman, learning to love in the everyday smog of life, learning to cry and smile in the same five minutes, to stumble and forgive, to help in tiredness and in strength, she will not ignore these dreams. They are the reality of a deep *hole* in her life.

It isn't enough to go through life stoically saying, "Life is full of holes." Hell, you've got to accept that hole, not spend yourself filling it up. To live and let life wash over it and cave it naturally in.

God, do you ever think that hole'll disappear?

No, not completely. You may learn to make love to life and God in a hundred different forms, but that hole'll never go. A virgin is an ill-concealed longing (talk like that sounds like someone's leaving the convent). So? In a life freely chosen there should be no shame in that. It's a longing for a tangible kingdom. Besides, longing is a form of prayer (thy kingdom come!). Since man first learned that he couldn't be satisfied with Eve or his garden, he has longed. *Surely you knew this, God. Why else did you choose winter to be born in?*

" 'Talk like that sounds like you're leaving the convent.' "

"She *said* that to you?" Sister Roberta licks her ice cream cone.

"Uh huh. But I'm going to make my vows for another year."

She looks at me. *"You are?"*

"Yeah. I'll need a year for it all to catch up. And Sister, I've got responsibilities—"

# Breaking the contract

"You do not make decisions in public, Sir, you make them alone, in your own little room . . . Don't—Don't ever forget that there are individuals who know what they want." Very deliberately.

"What do you want, Barbara?" Harold asks quietly.

"I want to go home—to return to the convent." There is little sound in the Mamas' and Papas' Game room. Mary watches me closely.

Harold Benjamin, the tribe leader, stretches out. He plays with his watch. "I haven't talked with you, Barbara, since your Trip—did you go through any changes?"

"Yes, I began to have a greater appreciation for what a man is and can become. I became more aware of how lovely it is to be a woman." Somebody guffaws; I glare. "And I gained respect for Synanon."

"And you're going to tell me—us—that you're going to let all that information go to waste?" Harold sits up.

"Of course not! If I didn't return to the convent it would be wasted—I'll share it with everyone I can."

"Who, Barb?" Mary inserts. "Your fifth-graders?"

"Mary, just because you're leaving the convent doesn't mean you have to misrepresent religious life. Like hell I only see fifth-graders," I toss her away.

She leans forward. "Okay—just how many men do you ever see?"

"Low blow, pal. You know, I don't see very many. But a woman's life—you know, Mary—her ability to be creative; well, it's not all bound up, necessarily, with a man."

She fumbles with a cigarette. "Really, Barb? Do you really believe that in your guts?"

Harold slaps his thigh. "Goddamn, this is the nicest contract Game I've ever witnessed!"

Carole, a petite brunette opens her mouth as wide as her body, "Assholes! For a moment, I thought you were going to be honest—going to *finally* break the contract!"

I smile across at Mary.

Nancy Clark looks at me hard. "God, Barbara, do you and Mary have your roles mixed up! I've never met anyone as sexually . . . alive as you. Skip Ferderber and I were just talking about it a few days ago. Yet here you are, giving us the nun-act, pretending you don't need a man to survive."

A woman yells, "Liar!"

"I don't, Nancy. Like I need love to survive but not necessarily a man."

Harold yawns. "Endless, fuckin' endless. It's Mary I'm interested in. Hey, Mary, you're going to stay at Synanon?"

She stiffens. "I'm not sure, but I *believe* in Synanon."

"What do you like here?"

She twitches. Leans forward; her voice is hoarse, intense. "What do I like? The children, the *fan*tastic community atmosphere we have here, the people—"

"Which kind of people?" Hal pushes it.

"Wha—what do you mean?"

"Men or women?"

"Why, the men of course!"

Harold smiles. "You know, Mary, you're really a beautiful girl. Were you as beautiful before you entered?"

Laughter. "Good God, that's a stupid question, Harold!" some man yells.

"All right, all right. I'm just trying to figure out why you'd ever enter—did you ever have problems with sex? Ever think you couldn't make it?"

Goodbye, Mamas and Papas. Isn't this where I came in? I watch Mary answering with her eyes, before she can make the words. She always was a pondering-woman. She smiles at him, "No—no problems."

"Bullshit! Bullshit, Mary," the words just bang out. "You're a fuckin' liar!" *Whoops.*

She almost knocks the ash tray over. "Wha—what are you talking about, Barbara?"

"I'm talking about how you said . . . God, Mary, I have to tell 'em."

"Wha*t*?" She bites down hard on the *t*.

"About how you said . . . remember, that night . . . you said"—I drop my voice—"you said that you might be—frigid."

They lean toward her. "Well?" Harold.

Mary's going to cry. "That's not how I meant it—oh, I'm so mixed up. I don't know anything anymore."

Nancy smiles at me. "So you did it."

"Did what?" I growl.

"Why, you broke your contract. Congratulations!"

No, baby, no congrats for cruelty. I did nothing extraordinary. I've been pulling Barbaraisms like that all my life. Just ask my Mom.

So even at Synanon we hand out medals for madness. To break a contract means to break an emotional tie with someone that has prevented you from being honest. Yet it's mad to be cruel. Mary. Don't we even have a right to the secret of our own doubts?

# *Protecting the family*

The underwear hangs exhausted on the towel rack. There's a mockingbird singing outside. Read to my kids in that *Green Laurels* book by Peattie that nightingales are Europe's bird, while whipperwills are ours. Hasn't been to California. Or at least not to Synanon. Right, Roberta? 'Tis the mockingbird.

And as I walk into the Club, there is the twenty-year-old kid I loaned my Kazantzakis' book to, the one who's been on speed since he was seventeen. He's sitting on the punk bench, his eyes burned out, his face sand-colored. They're going to drop him off at 'the end of the world'. His Adam's apple bobs in pain when I smile stupidly at him. What happened, what happened? Father Mike comes along, and drags my thoughts away from the boy.

"Special invitation to the children's Stew today, Barb?" he smiles.

"Yeah, wonder what we did?"

"Or, what he wants."

Al lights another cigarette. His mouth looks like someone took a handful of teeth and jabbed them in all at once. They probably have to fight to get brushed. He smiles at Mike and me.

"I invited you two in to share the Stew with the kids today. Are you wondering what we'll discuss?"

Nod.

Al turns to Mike Samson, another demonstrator at the School. "Turn the tape on." He flicks ashes off his blue and white striped farmer's overalls. "It'll be on 'Protecting the Family.' The point we're going to discuss is—the Church as a dishonest institution."

I stare at him. This is the first direct attack, besides the many innuendos, that Al has ever given us. I stretch out my legs. Well?

He begins with his usual toothy flourish. "Bucky Fuller has written that every Institution is an *environment*. Now the point here, Barbara, Mike, is the game you're playing. You know, don't examine the environment. It's the code of the street." He rises and quickly writes that on the board. Turns. "Or, in other words, don't cop out on your gang."

I look at him. "God, Al. Do you really believe that we don't examine our environment?"

Mike: "Yes. Haven't you heard of Vatican II?"

"Vatican Schmoo. Gobbledygook. The world is full of gobbledygook and the Church is part of the gobbledygook. The Church has hardening of the arteries." He writes the phrase on the board. "This, perhaps, is essential to its *staying power,* its inner consistency. And also, I suppose it lasts because it has a *limited sense of honesty.*"

Couldn't disagree with that. The Church is too big to expect some slender string of absolute honesty to stretch through all its bishops, priests, and people. "But," I protest, "it does have a slender thread of truth running through it."

Al smiles at me. "Truth? Where does *that* come from?"

"From my Lord. Jesus Christ."

He looks at me with his cold eyes. Very quietly. "Don't talk to me about Jesus Christ, nun. I probably know him better then you."

I shudder.

He looks at us again. "What is *life?* Is it the Church's version —a system for plugging dikes? Of course not. The integrity point for life has to be the doing." He draws a diagram on the board, and pontificates:

> Trust is the center of any doing. The belief that there are people who care that you exist. That you are a person to them and not coins for future steel and mortar adjuncts to a greater Institution.

"All right, Al," I begin. "I agree that it's in the doing that life comes. As Augustine once said, 'Let us run until we arrive—' "

"*Stop right there.* Bullshit," Al is yelling at me. "I don't want any of your poetry."

*Gulp. Stare.*

"And you're a pretty poor poet." My face must be melting

away. Damn that stupid poem I sent to him in the beginning. Why doesn't Mike say anything? Just like a priest—no balls.

Al continues. "But the point isn't that, Barbara. The point is—how willing are you to be uncomfortable in learning something?"

"What do you mean?" Mike asks.

"I mean that once you leave the code of your street, you're going to be uncomfortable. It'll hurt to cop out on your gang. But for an adult, it's an uncomfortableness that you can learn to live and grow with."

Afraid to try again. Must. "All right, Al. Dede said something a while back in the Stew that really hit me; he said that if Jesus came into Synanon, he would say, this is the place. Perhaps that's right, perhaps there's no place in this world as flexible or as able to accomplish real change in human beings—to heal."

"And really love them," Al adds (young sand-colored twenty-year-old seated on the punk bench. Do you still have my *Report to Greco?* Is this the way we love you? Saying "grow up" grow up grow up).

"But—why is there no worship at Synanon?" I ask. "No priests, rabbis, or ministers in any official capacity?"

He raises one eyebrow. Goes to the board. Writes, "Worship: worth." "Worship comes from the word 'to be worth.' We believe, Barbara, that all of Synanon is a form of worthiness before God and man." Al turns slightly to look at Mike Samson. "Interesting discussion, Mike?"

He rubs his hand over his bald head. "Yes, I suppose. As far as these discussions go."

Al sits down again. "So, Mike, speaking about cop-outs, I hear you were offered a thousand dollars."

Mike smiles shyly. *Watch out*, Mike, I want to say, my mind still ringing from Al's insult, *watch out*. "Yeah. They want me to film one of my short plays for them . . . I'll only be away one week," he adds.

Al sits down again. "Fuck it! When will you ever grow up, Mike Samson? First, we have to literally beg you to shave your head. Then to turn in your car. And last month? Remember last month?"

Mike bows his head. Yes, I remember. Hours browbeating

him because he wasn't teaching the kids correctly. They were bored. He hadn't even set up the radio shack yet. "But this is a good chance, Al. Synanon could sure use the money," Mike leans forward.

"Bullshit. I can lift up the phone right now and get ten times that! What you need is to stay here and do your work."

Mike slams his hand down, "*Bullshit* to that, Al Bauman. Always talking about the scholar and his needs—how do you know this might not be good for me?"

"Because I've read you, Mike Samson. I know what a child you are. I know—"

That old mockingbird, Synanon, singing again; that young sand-colored boy, gone; John Nicholas gone; probably Mike Samson, gone; you can't force anyone into the truth. It takes a lifetime to have it come.

I've got the urge to quit this Stew and go up to my workroom. Called in here to talk about honesty in the Church and all Al does is pontificate Synanon's position. But it's my fault. What's the Game for if you can't speak your mind? And my mind knows it wants to protect my family, the Church.

Here I've been trained to speak well of God and that "indestructable life within" (Hebrews) and I can't speak. Here I've chosen a life-style that exemplifies God's call "that we may all serve the living God" and I can't exemplify.

But, though I can't articulate it to Al, or to Synanon, I know unequivocably that belief in the Church means a passionate suffering and longing for the resurrection. Such passion frightens me. Can I bear such unrest and impatience to believe and demonstrate my belief in Jesus Christ?

I will be awkward all of my life, wiping my mouth with my hands until I die. And fall into holes and look at life from the distance that being in holes brings. I will reach for knowledge from holes—not knowing how to call, fearful of my own echo.

Fran. Why didn't I go talk to my soul-sister, Fran, when I was graceful, open?

# *Life's a f—*

They're mumbling toward me. Another Game like all the rest. They're putting up a motion picture screen before my face and seeing my eyes, running their movie of what I am, not listening to my words, but only hearing the canned heat of their own, preconceived thoughts about me, nun.

Me, nun, sitting in Titan Game. Soon I'll be going home. But have I helped anyone? Have I reached down and pulled someone out—out of what, I have no idea (perhaps God gives us ditches so that people like me, super-servers, can have something to do), but I know I've failed.

So, people, I'm going. *Can* your frayed tapes of this Barbie-nun—she's not going to be around.

"But, why in the hell are you leaving?"

Not so far from him now that I can't speak the tribe secretary Hector's language, "Because man, I gotta go."

"But what's the convent got?"

I smile. "That's like asking what anything that you love's got."

"Sonofabitch, I can tell you that—like my girl, she's got," he makes a smooth gesture with his hands and laughs, "and heroin, well, baby, it's good everytime . . . Hey . . . Is the convent your fix?"

I look at my hands. "I don't know . . . Perhaps God is my fix, sometimes—like, when prayer touches me and Him like fire . . ."

Two beautiful eyes bore through me. "Pr—prayer. What, what—how do you pray?"

I look at him. He's asking me to share my life with him—he really wants to know. God. If I could just shuffle through all this silt and find one good metaphor, just split one part of my soul for him to look in with his beautiful eyes and stutter—*wait, I'll be with you in just a sec—*

"What the hell, we can't wait all day," a newcomer yells. "Goddamn, prayer. I'll be a sonofabitch! Are you turning this game into a bullshitting, I do repeat, bullshitting cerebration, Hector!"

"Well, Sam, the games are changing now—look at the Stews! They use to be hate/smash/kill—now they're—"

"You're cocksucking these people, boy! This ain't no Stew, Hector! It's just a few minutes where these boys and girls can dump their shit and you're sitting here, pulling it along at a leisurely pace."

"Shut up!" I yell. *I've missed my chance, and I know it.* "What do you know about these people and their needs? Because the Game stills down a bit, and one human being asks another human being a simple question, hell, you'd think we'd used a needle."

He smiles at me. "You have, baby, you have—you see, honey-hole nun, you can touch on any of your goddamn religion any ol' time you want, but screw you! We've got some new people in here who'd like to shove the whole works and use that needle. And your Goddamn, sonofabitch quiet talk might just force them to." He winks at the room. "And honey-hole, don't you think they've heard all that shit before? Prayer, goddamn!"

Hector shuffles a bit, looks around the room for someone to put the Game on. Just got to get it off the nun. Sees a huge black man in the corner. "Ah—hey, John, that your name, boy?"

"Yeh, mon, John is ma name."

"How long ya been here?"

"Five days mon—"

"You'd like a little somethin' right now?"

"Sure, mon—" His cracked teeth show in a grin, a grimace. "Life's a fuck, mon . . . I'd like me a little lady or a wee fix."

An undercurrent, low: "Both, baby, *both*."

A puffed-up blond drummer who plays in the Sounds of Synanon Band asks, "Why have you stayed this long, John?"

"I dunno, mon . . . I'd been thinkin' I might split—soon—but I don' think so."

"Why not?"

"Because—well, mon," he shifts carefully in his chair, "I'd like to wake up one morning with not de needle upon me, with not de woman layin' on my mind." He touches the center of his forehead, ". . . I'd like to go down and play de paddle tennis, see, mon, and lay on de sand and be happy again."

*"Asshole!"* the blond sneers. "Do you think you'll ever reach a point when it'll be like that? I've been here five months, now, yet I still wanta split." He grabs the side of his chair. "Sure, Goddamn, they even let me, five months in, go up to S.F. and play with the band at the Street Scene . . . I walk around and the Directors pat me on the back. And I know *it's all bullshit,* all crap—man, I haven't changed a bit."

Hector: "Hey, Fred, what's with you today?"

"I'm just goin' crazy, that's all! Your Goddamn six months' fucking ban!" His face is white.

Someone laughs. "So you've got a girl friend?"

Fred rubs his upper lip. "Yeah. Yeah. I've got a girl and I don't want to be held back." He grips that chair again, ". . . all I want to do, all I really ever want to do—"

Someone, low: "Say it, baby. Go on—"

*"Fuck. Fuck. Fuck."* He slams his hands down. "That's all I really want to do!"

Me, nun, frozen in the hard chair. From prayer to this? But somehow, I feel strong. Yeah. Strong. Like the time I went to visit an old friend in a Carmelite monastery in San Diego. Mary had finally made up her mind she was going to leave the convent as soon as our Synanon experience was over, and I felt, forgive the acquired Synanonese, like Sister Shit. I wanted the other people I was with to cut the irrelevant questions. Surely this silent freckled nun in the floppy brown and white outfit must have the answers.

"Do you pray much?" I asked her.

"What do you mean?" she giggles.

"I mean, how long do you pray?"

"Long enough," she giggles again, nervously moving her extensive Carmelite habit.

"Of course, she prays all the time," someone says.

"Do you have spiritual conversations?" I ask.

She laughs out loud. "What do you mean?"

I lift my eyes, still hoping. "I mean do you talk about *God?"*

"Yes—sometimes—I don't know."

The conversation goes back to Church gossip, Jackie Kennedy, somebody's second cousin married somebody else's brother, and my Carmelite begins to come alive.

Interrupt again. "Why do people have to suffer, Sister?" (Why does Mary have to leave me? Why in the hell do we have to be so sad? Surely you know, baby, *you know.*)

"I—we—what do you mean?" she giggles again. Over a year she's been in this place, knocking on God's door. If she doesn't know the answer, who does?

Later, when we were all leaving, she called me over to the grill. She held onto one bar tightly and said, "I'm sorry, I couldn't . . . It didn't seem the place . . . I haven't seen you for so long."

I looked at her. Baby, if this isn't the place, then I don't know where is the place. So, "It's all right, Sister. I forgot you don't talk much." (*But Mary, sadness, what am I going to do?*)

"No . . . I don't talk much . . . I'm so sorry."

"Of course." Tears. Now spit it out: "But don't forget there's people dying outside."

She holds onto those damn bars. "I know—dying . . . I *do* think about it, perhaps all the time."

No answer. But I felt better; just wanted her to remember. Wanted to see the memory on her face. Hard and cracked. Because that's what we are, baby.

Thanks, Synanon. It's not that my Carmelite friend is wrong. There's nothing stupid in spending your life knocking on God's door, if it's for others. But if your motivation isn't others, baby, you're missing something powerful. Purity isn't the essence of life, because nothing we want is ever pure—who's ever tried to work a dream out? Does a dream stay in a nice white pocket; does it come out clean, fresh, untouched by human failure? Does it? No, mon, it don't. Like the black man says, heaven is to wake up one morning with not de needle upon me, with not de woman layin' on my head.

And who's got the right to heaven right now? Who's ever got the right to close the door against life? Don't tell me that life's the early rising with the morning star hanging in your breast and the night watching with the moon flecking your eyes. It's not being pure in a wooden choir loft. Life's always a Goddamn longing, a freeway.

But I'm not saying you're wrong, Carmelite friend. I'm not knocking your right to God—there are mysteries in life that don't belong to words. What I'm saying (has someone said this to me before?) . . . *Life's a fuck, mon.*

Me, nun, sitting frozen in a wooden chair. From prayer to this?

# *Four days 'til salvation*

The nuns sat in the different places assigned to them in Chapel and stared dumbly ahead. What was there to do the rest of their days except avoid salvation?

"That's what you all think it's like, don't you?" I smile to myself a little grimly. "God, if you only *knew!*"

Then Carole of the ample mouth takes another drag, and continues her story, "Finally, he left Synanon and wanted to come home."

Someone: "Of course, you didn't let him—you know Synanon's view on *that.*"

An old lady asks, "But why, why? If the child can't make it at Synanon, isn't it cruel to cut him off from his parents?"

A blond woman, shaking slightly, "The child's got to grow up. He's got to stand on his own two feet. The best thing Carole can do for her son is to slam the door in his face."

A reaction. Carole, softly, "But the father gives in to him."

A blond woman named Val retorts, "Then the father will destroy him."

"What do you mean?"

"I mean this happened with our son. He started on marijuana, then he was on pills." She wipes the back of her neck with her hand. "The police picked him up three times but the damn courts didn't jail him."

"Why not?"

"The courts'll protect the kid until it's too late. Every goddamn time we took him back. His father even gave him *money.* Then the last time he got busted."

"How, dear?" The old woman asks.

"He broke into a drugstore."

Carole seems to understand. "Val," she says, "you don't have to go on—you don't have to finish it."

Val waves her aside. "I'm doing it for my benefit as well as yours—the boy hated jail. He kept begging us to take him out. For once in our lives we wouldn't . . ." she muffles her face in her hands, "we wouldn't give in. It was too late. One night he took off his belt and strangled himself." Her head falls forward into her hands.

No one moves, and the old lady begins to wail. Why do women choose wailing as the last recourse? Most do—they crumple and cry. But Synanon—it can work with kids if they're allowed to be free of their parents. It's like a Novitiate. Its use of recreation, motion, vacuum, pressure, role modeling, learning, talk (its particular form of prayer), self-reliance, all tend to make a man more worthy. And Al *is* right, worship is worthiness.

If that woman—Val—if she'd cut her umbilical cord from that boy so that he *could* have returned to Synanon, perhaps he would have lived. She didn't and he died. She passes on her hell to us.

"We're going to miss you, Sister Barbara," the fat man smiles at me, glad to change the atmosphere.

"Yes, dear," the old woman perks up, "you've certainly given us a lot of laughs."

"By the way, are you still a virgin?" Harriet asks.

I laugh. "Yes."

"Do you have time before you go back?" The woman moves a little in her chair.

I gulp. "Time for what?"

"Well—can't you change *all* that before you return?"

We laugh.

"God, lady. I've only got four days left."

*"Well?"*

# The kingdom between night and sleep

Well. The longing sits upon my head. I fold my hands, lay me down to sleep, and this is the dream I have:

But where *is* His kingdom?

It's a home.

But where, *where* is this house?

It's in a very deep place.

*How* deep?

When you lie awake at night, do you look out your window? Do you see white holes in the sky?

Yeah. So you've seen them, too?

Yes. I've seen them.

Is *that* where His home is?

Yes. It's on the edge of the night and your sleep.

I don't understand.

Do you believe in the night?

Uh huh. I think so.

Do you believe life dies in the night?

No. I *know* flowers always grow.

Do you believe you die when you sleep?

You just asked me that.

All right. Have you ever been in bed with the night upon you and your sleep seeping into it?

I don't understand.

(I took His face in mine.) Neither do I. But I believe His kingdom is somewhere between the night and our sleep. And that *that* hole is utterly creative. That all the knocks we may have to take somehow widen that hole. Then one day (I clap my hands) we'll just joyfully slip into his kingdom.

(He laughs.) Will it be a warm home? With a fireplace?

Sure. Flowers on every polished wooden table.

Candles?

Oh, yes. Chocolate cream pies everywhere.

Green fields?

Yes. But the best part—

What? What?

The lamb will invite the lion for dinner. And He'll be invited too.

Will it be a long time until His kingdom, Sister?

(Sister. I looked at him softly and then outside to the beach.) I don't know. (And a veil came between us. I didn't speak. We watched the sea and the sea. And the sea.)

# *The environment of wonder*

August, I think. The locks click open. This is what I want to remember: it is Saturday and Al is wearing his favorite light-blue jacket, Ivy League shirt, light pants, and blue socks with tennis shoes. A man whose clothes say yes. We members of the School Staff sit in the kid's Stew room. Al's got his cigarettes, his blackboard. He snaps his lighter open, lights a cigarette, and begins.

"The old teaching methods had the structure of an ego performer. You know, get a captive audience and do your thing . . . There is something in the very nature of a teacher that is akin to tap dancing. The audience sits in awe as you do your dance. This may be very fine—but do you know how many routines the best tap dancers know?"

We look at one another. "Ten?" I say.

"The finest tap dancers," he smiles at me, "have a repertoire of four steps. This is not what we want at Synanon. We don't want limitation."

Vicki raises her eyebrow at me.

"Our central focus here is communication, and the character of our teaching. We need and must have scholars on our staff. Scholars—that is, demonstrators of *learning*." He takes a drag of his cigarette. "This is important. Here the teaching function (you know, methods, lesson plans, busy work, ideas) is subsidiary to the *discovering* function."

He picks up a piece of chalk. He writes "A Sharing" on the board. "Teaching is only a by-product of discovery. It is a sharing of the delights."

He sits down again, and leans back with his head cradled in his arms. "A scholar, it seems to me, is someone who discovers something. He is someone who is delighted with the time and space to do it in. Only one thing is asked of the scholar here at Synanon—share your thinking process. Don't do it for us. But show us how you come to the point of discovery."

Al claps his hands. "Do you realize what this means? It *is*

Synanon. Teaching becomes a role—modeling process—one follows not just ideas, but a person—a life-style of learning!"

He rises. "But you can see the problem. As Goodman says in *Community of Scholars,* the real problem is the motivation of scholars, not the motivation of students." He tosses the chalk up and down. "A scholar is delighted with the time and space to discover in. We have set up the environment for scholars—what more does a discoverer need than room, paper, pencil, and the Pacific Ocean?"

I cough at Vicki. If only his promise of time and silence were true. But Synanon has a thing with time: stealing it from you, as all hungry human beings steal time and silence.

"The environment must give the sense of a scholar at work. Your room should be expressive of yourselves. It should say 'Come in,' though not necessarily to anyone else but yourselves."

He sits down and puts his legs out. "What does it mean? It doesn't necessarily mean a harder act *as if*—but rather, it's a matter of shifting the positions . . . What really do we want from you? That quality of enthusiasm that the child will remember. What is your obligation? It is the obligation of the scholar passing on information. The child will come to you and say: how do you do it? And your job is to share, to show him the tools *you* use to help *your* sense of discovery. So what must you do right now?"

His brown eyes burn around the room. "A teacher says and thinks, 'How do I get this piece of information across?' But a scholar is centered. First, think who you are and, then, share your discovery. It is like what Nijinsky said before he danced; 'I am Nijinsky. I *am* Nijinsky.' And then he could go out and be the Firebird."

He smiles to himself. "Adam, my son, hated public school. I think the teachers disliked him, too." He chuckles. "He sat all wound around his desk, yawning away, staring into the dark forests of the mind—the teachers would fidget on their platform. *How dare he!* They'd pounce upon him, and you know what?" He smiles. "He'd always get the answer right. He *was* listening, but not *their* way. The enthusiasm for performing is registered by clapping and face reaction. Perhaps the enthusiasm for learning is boredom? Who knows? But I do know your performance: it is to discover in public."

He clicks his lighter shut. I wish it were true, Al. I came to Synanon willing to dance for free. You gave me the Pacific Ocean, pencil and paper. Like I said earlier, you gave me much more, but it wasn't enough.

What *has* Synanon done for you, my deah? When a person is nineteen, it's easy for him to believe that he is a revolutionary, a prophet, or a saint. When he turns twenty-three, he becomes satisfied with the small. Love is small. It is the sign of a root.

Of course I'm still twenty-two.

# Goodbye, kids, goodbye, pigeons

"Don't you go layin' that shit about feeling twenty-two for the first time, Al. Hell, I'm the one who told you that anyway!"

"All right, let's follow it. What responsibilities and risks are you going back to in your fucking convent, Sister Asshole? What decisions concerning love do *you* make? You think you're so mature? *Bullshit!* Think of the young married women your own age."

"Bullshit to that! A lot of my age group are divorced! Here at Synanon and elsewhere. Don't trip me, Al Bauman: I know this, that one takes the highest risk and greatest responsibility when one chooses to serve God. *You know* there is no greater risk than the possibility of losing oneself."

He takes a drag from his cigarette. I'm shivering. All the children are with us. Goodbye, kids. Goodbye, pigeons. My gut is unfastened today. Soon it'll float up to my heart.

"Look, Al," I begin again quietly. "I'll always have the greatest respect for what you're doing here. I've been inside the shell. I know it's good inside, it works . . . It works fine for dingbats. It works for teenage kids who need direction. It maybe even works for emotionally fucked-up adults. But, goddamn, I've gone through one Novitiate, I'd be a *fool* to go through another."

"How do you know? You've barely come out of your cocoon, Barbara." He rubs his forehead.

I touch *my* forehead. "I know. It'll just take a while for the answers to work out in my life."

One of the girls, Kathy, asks, "How long?"

I smile. "About a year." I turn back to Al. "But that doesn't mean I'll come back."

He jabs his cigarette into the air. "You *need* Synanon, kid."

The kids start yelling at me. "Yeah, we need you!" "Please stay, Barbara." "Proud ass!"

I'm trying to nail my gut down. I'll not cry in front of these kids.

"Look, I've lived in boarding schools, community life

(religious), and Synanon. I know what it takes to change a boarding school, when people live together for convenience, into a community. It takes *esprit de corps*."

Kenny: "Eh? What?"

Al: "The spirit that holds a group together."

"Right," I say. "For us Sisters, it's God. Otherwise every convent in the world would disintegrate. Women are not meant to live together—except for God. But here—I've been thinking about this a lot, Al."

For the first time, he smiles at me. "Yes, Barbara. I want to hear," he says.

Turning into liquid, I continue: "The *esprit de corps* at Synanon is weakness. The weak helping the weak to become strong—human—self-reliant. Once that happens, Al—once a person becomes strong, you should rejoice! I mean, eventually the training will take hold and they'll grow up—and they'll leave."

"But Synanon's more than a place for the weak. It's a social movement."

"Sure it is. But there's some people who need more freedom than you could ever give." All right, Barb, pull yourself together. Linda notices. She hands me a Kleenex.

Al leans forward. "Some of the kids have been invited to the circus today, Barbara. We'll have to end this. Would you see Dede before you leave?"

Sure. "Sure, Al." I'm floating away.

For once, Al is awkward. "Er," he stammers, "you've done a good job here, Barbara. You're a fine teacher. We appreciate—"

The kids start hugging me. Nora, Adam, Kenny, Susie, Alex, Kathy, goodbye.

I go up to my workshop. Kenny follows me up. I wipe my nose.

He doesn't seem to notice. "Will you read me *Wrinkle in Time?* Huh? huh? you promised."

"Sure, I'll read you *Wrinkle in Time.*" Although the words and my heart are blurring. Then we clean up my room. I hand him a stool from the Planetarium room to take upstairs. Over to the main house to find Dede, but he's not in yet. As I come back, I meet Kenny. His lips are rolling under and his face is dark. I can hear the pigeon's aching chant, always the basso continuo to this summer.

Kenny doesn't look at me. He walks past. I watch him turn the corner by the main house. I follow him. There, behind a high shrub he and I rock in each other's arms.

"Don't go, Barbara, please don't go. Stay here . . . Stay here with us. I don't want you to go," he chants, and the pigeons and English sparrows chant it with him.

Just the other day, Dorothy Salant showed us a Sierra Club film on Glen Canyon in the Colorado River. Somewhere near Lee's Ferry is a huge cave. When Powell took a small boat down the Colorado, he wrote that this cave could hold 50,000 people easily; an enormous natural amphitheater. But the narrator of the film said, as we watched three lonely shadows walk into the cave, "Let there be places built for 50,000 people but let this huge cave remain for the few people who seek it out . . ."

Let this huge cave remain, Kenny, for the few people who seek it out.

Later in the movie we saw insects, flowers, and birds. The narrator said, "Some flowers are meant to be seen and used. But it is not wrong for a few flowers to be left alone . . . Alone, for perhaps no one to notice except a huge cave, a few insects, some birds—and the few who seek them out."

Don't know why I have to leave, Kenny. Maybe I'm just meant for a life of searching, and what to most people will seem uselessness.

"I love you, Kenny," I said, touching his tanned face. "And I wish I could be content with Synanon, but I've got something else to do." If the wind knew anything about longing, it would suck up the world.